SPELLS
DICTIONARY

SPELLS
DICTIONARY

EVERYTHING YOU NEED TO KNOW
ABOUT SPELLS AND ENCHANTMENTS
TO BRING MAGIC INTO YOUR LIFE

COMPREHENSIVE EXPLANATIONS
OF SPELL CRAFT, FROM MAGICAL
POWDERS AND POTIONS TO
TALISMANS AND CHARMS

Antonia Beattie

THUNDER BAY
P · R · E · S · S
SAN DIEGO, CALIFORNIA

If this be magic, let it be an art.

—WILLIAM SHAKESPEARE

CONTENTS

INTRODUCTION

Using spells to empower your life

Spells have been a part of life since the earliest days of human existence. There are literally countless spells—some recorded on paper and others passed down by word of mouth—designed to help attract love, luck, and popularity. There are also spells that help protect you, your family, and your friends from misfortune.

There are good spells and bad spells. This book is concerned with good spells—spells that can be safely performed and that will benefit you, your family, and your friends. Bad spells, spells that try to harm people or make them do things against their will, are dangerous. First, casting a spell intended to harm is not a decent thing to do, and second, bad spells attract three times the amount of negative energy they send out.

There are many different types of spells. Some use traditional words or phrases that have evolved over centuries. Others use traditional tools, such as colored candles. None of the tools used in spell casting is expensive or difficult to obtain.

The spells and charms in this book all use readily available ingredients and tools—herbs, candles, needles, thread, crystal, and other things you probably already have. You won't need a lot of space, time, and money to create your spells, but you will need faith in yourself and a deep inner belief that you can achieve your desired goals.

Spells are often a mixture of words, objects, and actions. They are chosen because their combined vibrations tune into your purpose. For example, if you want to find a new love, you would traditionally use a red candle, patchouli oil, rose quartz, and the petals of a red rose. By focusing on preparing the spell and by saying a series of words over and over again, you will create a powerful spell to find a new love.

Over many centuries, various stones, animals, birds, trees, plants, and colors have been given certain magical meanings. These are sometimes called associations or correspondences; the *Spells*

Dictionary will give you some of the most common correspondences for various spells.

Spell casting is a very simple and direct approach to getting what you want—it is merely a way of collecting, raising, and directing energy. Many people believe that there is a great amount of psychic energy circulating in our bodies and that this energy is compatible with the psychic energy of the Earth. Spell craft is essentially Earth magic. Spells help you tap into the psychic energy that is within you—and within the Earth—and harness it to create a new reality where your wish will become real.

Casting a spell is like sending out a flare of energy that will attract happiness, popularity, or some other positive outcome to you. Spells are a kind of extra push—they will make things happen in your favor and rearrange the type of energy that is flowing to you.

If what you want feels beyond your reach, spells can help bring opportunities to you, and then you can follow these to your desired goal. They can also help give you the ability to recognize opportunities and are an excellent way of strengthening your intuition.

However, spell craft should not be used as a substitute for doing all you can physically and mentally to make something that you want happen in your life. Doing such everyday things is part of your own personal magic, and can help you gather information that will make your spell casting even more powerful and successful.

THE FINE ART OF SPELL CRAFT

Some important magical rules

One of the most important skills for successful spell casting is concentration. You need to be able to focus on the success of your spell. If you are looking for a job, for instance, imagine an envelope with a nice healthy paycheck inside.

Test your concentration skills with the following visualization exercise. Do this exercise before doing any of the spells in this book—it will help you focus your power toward your spell.

Sit comfortably on the floor or ground, close your eyes, and imagine that you are a tree. The first step is to concentrate on your spine. Start from the base and work up, bit by bit, to the base of your skull, feeling the flow of energy through your body. Imagine that your spine is illuminated in a golden light. Then turn that golden light into a golden trunk of a tree.

Visualize the base of your golden trunk extending downward into the Earth. Let your mind drift free as you watch the roots grow and spread, anchoring your body into the Earth. Imagine your branches rising up, then turning and flowing gracefully down, like those of a willow tree, to touch the ground.

Feel the energy pulsing through you. Feel yourself capable of doing anything you want. When you're ready, shut down the color and focus on your breathing. After a while the image of the tree will fade, but the feeling of being connected will remain. When you are connected to the Earth, you are able to fulfill your potential.

Spells don't work if you have a deep-seated feeling that you don't deserve the things you want. For quicker results, consider working with a group of friends, casting spells for each other. For longer lasting results, work out how to get rid of any such self-defeating feelings and discover your own individual path to happiness.

Remember, always follow or create spells that are for your benefit or for someone you care about. If you do hurt someone with your spell, even without meaning to, you may have to deal with negative karma. Karma is an Eastern concept of paying for the wrong you do to others. The same thing happens in Western magic: whatever is sent out returns in time upon the sender. In magic, the formula is said to be "that which is sent out returns threefold."

Sometimes it is legitimate to cast a spell that will prevent someone from doing harm to others. White witches have been known to work such magic when it is thought to be for the greater good. However, there is always a price to be paid. During World War II, a group of witches cast spells to prevent Hitler from invading England. A worthy purpose, but some of the witches who were involved in the spells died soon after the ritual. They were quite elderly, and some feel that they were willingly making the ultimate sacrifice for their country.

It is also important not to force anyone to do your bidding. You are wasting a lot of energy if the person is not interested. It needs a lot of energy to actually pull off such a spell—this is possibly why past magicians needed to call up spirits to coerce the person into showing the proper interest. However, these magicians usually had to pay a heavy price—these spirits tended to charge quite heavily for their services.

SPELL CRAFT TIP

Spells work best when they are performed after you have:
- Worked out exactly what you want to do
- Imagined the changes in detail
- Allowed yourself to be guided by your intuition and personal knowledge
- Convinced yourself that you can make a difference

Preparing yourself for spell craft

To prepare yourself for successful spell casting, clear your mind of everyday thoughts and anxieties by taking a bath or shower.

If you are taking a shower, stand directly under the shower head and imagine your body being encased by the water, which is removing all the troubles, unhappiness, and thoughts of the day. At this point, do not even think about your spell. What you need to do is clear your mind and get a sense of stillness. Watch the water swirling down the drain together with your everyday worries.

If you are taking a bath, do a cleansing visualization with a lighted candle while lying in the bathtub. Place a beeswax candle or tea light so that it can be safely and easily seen from the bathtub. Place a large glass of cool water where you can easily reach from the tub.

As you soak in the water (into which you have dropped some sea salt and a drop or two of an essential oil), take the time to feel your senses. Check the taste in your mouth, taking a sip of water if you feel a little thirsty. Notice the scent of the oils you have chosen, create little waves in your tub with your hands and listen to the motion of the water, and feel how the hot and cold water mingle and caress your skin. When you are ready, get out of the bath or the shower and dry yourself

AROMATHERAPY OIL	QUALITIES
cedarwood	stabilizes emotions
geranium	cleanses emotions
lavender	attracts calmness
lovage	attracts love
marjoram	relieves grief
peppermint	overcomes shock
sandalwood	stimulates confidence
vervain/verbena	attracts lover
ylang ylang	relieves depression

with a fresh towel. If you had a bath, let the water out and watch the water and all your worries go down the drain.

Go directly to the place where you are going to do your spell—your spell room. If you are feeling jittery or unsettled, set up a full-length mirror in your spell room and do the following exercise, which will help you feel more grounded and together.

Stand in front of the mirror with your feet together. Let your shoulder blades drop, your shoulders straighten, and your chest rise, freeing any constriction on your diaphragm. Check particularly how your back feels. If your lower back feels stressed while standing, tilt your pelvis slightly forward. You will find that your knees will unlock and bend slightly.

Look at yourself in the mirror. Imagine a line of energy running through the middle of your body. Visualize that line of energy going down your legs, through your feet, and into the ground under the floor. Then imagine another line of energy coming up from the Earth into your body. Visualize these lines of energy mingling and strengthening. This is called grounding.

Use the mirror to help you straighten your body along this central line of energy. Without moving your limbs, imagine all the muscles in your body moving toward this center, balancing your body. When you are feeling centered, move away from the mirror and read through the spell you are going to do, visualizing its success. You are now ready for some serious spell craft!

SPELL CRAFT TIP

Reconnecting with the Earth for spell craft power

When we feel ugly, stupid, or socially undesirable, most times this means that our energy is disconnected from the Earth. When you feel like this, try to do the exercise above, even if you are not planning to do any spells. It is important to stay connected with the Earth—it helps get rid of feelings of depression and unhappiness.

Preparing your space for spell craft

The best place to do your spell casting is an area—a spell room—that is quiet, protected from interruptions and separated from the bustle of everyday life. Once you have selected your spell area, whether it is your bedroom, study, workshop, or in the garden, set up a little table there, upon which you can place some flowers, candles, incense, and a bowl half full of sand. Make sure the table is big enough for your spell ingredients, this book and perhaps a spell journal, where you can record any insights or curious occurrences that take place during or after your spell casting.

Set this area aside for spell casting and make sure no clutter builds up there. People in a number of ancient civilizations believed that clutter slows down the energy circulating around your space. If clutter does become a problem, hang or place a clear quartz crystal where the clutter is worst, and let the stone clear the energy in the area and remind you to keep the space tidy. Keeping your spell room clear of clutter will have a corresponding effect in your life and on your ability to focus.

Before you do any spell casting, you will need to cleanse your spell room of negative energy. Mix a teaspoon of sea salt with a cup of water and sprinkle it around the edges of the room, spiraling inward until you reach the area's center. Sprinkle the salty water at the doorway, windows, and ventilation grates; doing this may discourage disturbances from other members of the family or from people dropping in.

SPELL CRAFT TIP
Visualizing a protective circle

To protect your space, cast a circle of imaginary blue light right around the room. Do this when you are feeling vulnerable or upset. Always make sure that you cut a doorway in the light so that you can walk in and out of your room. If you have had a really unsettling argument with someone in your room, burn some incense or a calming essential oil, such as lavender, to clear the air of negative energy from the argument. Ring a melodious-sounding bell in each corner of your room to further clear the air.

Decorate the area with your favorite fabrics and objects. Images of stars and moons, plus beads, lush fabrics, feathers, and lots of candles should make this a special space to retreat to. You can also use this space for meditating and for your visualization exercises.

Over the centuries, many people have found that bringing something that represents nature into their home makes them feel a little more connected to the energy of the Earth—seeing how vast this power is can help us put some of our problems into perspective.

Consider decorating your spell room as a cavern of wonder and delight, a haven where you can escape the troubles and pressures of the everyday world. Use pictures and fabrics that remind you of the natural world—as many as possible—to allow you to link into its wonder and its power.

Use as much natural fabric as you can in your decorations (for your spell room and your bedroom). If you are into crafts, make some pictures, covers for your bed, and small boxes or ornaments; they will also remind you how clever you are with your hands. Having your personal space full of objects and pictures that you have made yourself creates a powerful haven to help you regenerate your strength.

To remind you of the natural world, set up a small table in your bedroom or spell room and on it place some candles, incense, your favorite stones and gems, and small pictures of your favorite people.

Timing your spells

The moon, the position of the planets, and the cycles of nature have a lot to do with the timing of your spells. During a full moon is traditionally one of the most effective times to do any type of magic—it is thought that the fullness of the moon relates to a raised level of spiritual energy, which can be harnessed for spell casting.

During a full moon is the time for healing spells and for making charm bags to attract love and protection. It is also a good time to cut any herbs you may be growing for your spells. The phase of a new moon is a perfect time to seek inspiration and guidance about a new project, relationship, or career. Spells that deal with the ending of things, such as relationships or a job, should be done during the waning of the moon (when the moon's light is decreasing).

While it is often effective to rely on your intuition when you are choosing the right day for your spell, there are also some traditional

correspondences you may find helpful. Use the table below to work out which day and ruling planet correspond to the particular type of spell you wish to cast—these energies will power your spell to success.

Another way of working out when to cast your spell is to find out what zodiac sign the moon is in each day. Each zodiac sign has its own energy, and you can tap into

DAY	PLANET	TYPE OF SPELL
Sunday	Sun	spells to gain insight
Monday	Moon	spells to understand your dreams
Tuesday	Mars	spells to protect yourself from your enemies
Wednesday	Mercury	spells to help you pass your exams
Thursday	Jupiter	spells to acquire wealth and money
Friday	Venus	spells to attract love or friendship
Saturday	Saturn	spells to protect your home or business

this energy to power your spell. As it passes through each sign, the moon's energy is affected by the qualities of that constellation.

This relationship between the moon and the zodiac sign is not related to the phases of the moon, but corresponds with which part of the sky the moon is in. There are many astrological or moon calendars or diaries available, as well as guides on the Internet—all you have to do is look up one of these guides.

The table below lists the different energies that are generated by the moon while it is in a particular astrological phase.

MOON AND ZODIAC SIGN	TYPE OF ENERGY	EXAMPLE OF A TYPE OF SPELL
Moon in Aries	energy, new projects, independence, protection (when you have been involved in an argument), desire, competition	spell to protect yourself from being drained in an argument
Moon in Taurus	prosperity, security, affection, artistic and musical talents, resources, nature, quality	spell to open your creativity
Moon in Gemini	adaptability, intelligence, communication, transportation, choices, learning	spell to help you with your studies
Moon in Cancer	home and family, the past, intuition, safety and protection, healing and nurturing	spell to let go of a painful past
Moon in Leo	children, creativity, courage, strength and vitality, romance, recognition, leadership	spell to attract popularity
Moon in Virgo	organization, health, perfection, gardening, pets, attention to details, skills	spell to help you finish your school assignments
Moon in Libra	love, attraction, justice, balance, beauty, decoration, socializing, partnerships	spell to attract a new love or friend
Moon in Scorpio	secrets, intuition, emotions, passion, intensity, psychic skills, endings and beginnings	spell to help you end a relationship
Moon in Sagittarius	travel, study, confidence, optimism, success, good fortune, adventure	spell to help you study
Moon in Capricorn	responsibility, achievement, structure, authority, commitment, wisdom, reputation	spell to help you commit to a relationship
Moon in Aquarius	originality, freedom, new ideas, friends, groups, change, unconventional	spell to help you stand up for yourself
Moon in Pisces	spirituality, imagination, psychic abilities, dreams, compassion, healing, escape	spell to help your friend

SIMPLE SPELL CRAFT TOOLS

Candles

Candles are one of the simplest tools in spell craft. Wax has traditionally been used for magic because of its ability to absorb magical intention. Differently colored and shaped candles can be used for virtually any type of spell. Candles can also help spell casters focus on their wish. Once the candle is burned, it is believed, the spell caster's magical wish is released into the cosmos.

In most candle magic spells, you must use a candle of a particular color, and you must first dress or anoint it with some scented oil. Wax can also be carved or engraved easily, so you can carve symbols or words on the candle to help dedicate it to your magical wish. You might carve the magic symbol for Jupiter $2\!\!\!/$ or a simplified picture of a fat and happy dragon if you are casting a money magic spell, for instance.

If you are using candles in your spell craft, first wash your candle in salted water to get rid of any stray negative energy. Dry the candle thoroughly, wrap it in some cotton (preferably the same color as the candle), and leave it in the light of the moon overnight. Select whichever oil suits your type of spell and rub a couple of drops of it into the candle. Almond oil is a

---

SPELL CRAFT TIP

Don't reuse your candles for a new spell

Don't use candles that are half burned down for your spell. Use a fresh candle for every spell unless you want to repeat the spell you have just done exactly. In that case, wrap the unused part of your candle in a cloth made of natural fiber, with a note reminding you of the spell you used it with.

COLOR OF CANDLE	CORRESPONDING MEANING	CORRESPONDING OIL
red	love	patchouli
pink	friendship	mugwort
orange	courage	endive
green	money	cinnamon
yellow/gold	confidence	basil
blue	calm	chamomile
purple	power	frankincense

good all-purpose oil substitute if you don't have any aromatherapy oils or if you are using a scented candle.

The color of the candle and the oil it is dressed with are usually determined by the purpose of your spell. See the table above for some traditional associations. However, if these do not feel right for you, use a plain beeswax candle or meditate quietly on what color would best suit your purpose.

The shape of your candle is also important. Spherical candles are useful for spells involving your emotions. They should be left to burn overnight in a small metal bowl filled with sand—the sand will catch the falling wax.

For other types of spells, such as those about money and confidence, use upright candles—the usual tapering ones or those shaped like an obelisk. These candles can also be left to burn overnight, but if you want a concentrated burst of energy to power your spell, it is common to stick a pin or needle toward the top of the candle and focus your intention on the candle while it burns down to the pin or needle. Once the flame touches the pin or needle, the power of the spell is released.

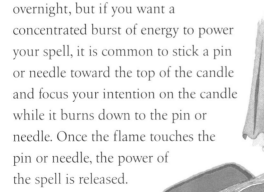

Cords, fabric, and thread

It is important to use only natural objects in spells, because they hold magical power much more easily than objects made of artificial substances such as nylon and plastic. Fabric is often used in the making of charm bags or the storing of magical tools. Try to use only cotton, silk, hemp, and other natural fabrics. The same holds true for thread—use only cotton or silk thread.

Some of the most effective spells use cord magic. For this type of magic, all you need is a length of rope or cord into which you can knot your magical intention. The action of knotting a cord is supposed to anchor your wish into the cord, making the knot a symbol of your wish becoming a reality.

Wearing certain garments while doing a spell can help you feel empowered and able to make a difference in your own life. Do you have a dress, shirt, robe, or other garment that makes you feel good, as if you are protected? A garment that you can pull

---

TRADITIONAL SPELL

Take a cord long enough to be knotted nine times—the length you need will depend on the thickness of your cord. Say the following words and make your knots according to the patterns below, while concentrating on the success of your spell:

By knot of one, the spell's begun.	✳
By knot of two, it comes true.	✳ ✳
By knot of three, so mote it be.	✳ ✳ ✳
By knot of four, power I store.	✳ ✳ ✳ ✳
By knot of five, the spell is alive.	✳ ✳ ✳ ✳ ✳
By knot of six, the spell is fixed.	✳✳✳ ✳ ✳ ✳
By knot of seven, events I'll leaven.	✳✳✳ ✳ ✳✳✳
By knot of eight, it will be fate.	✳✳✳✳✳ ✳✳✳
By knot of nine, what is done is mine.	✳✳✳✳✳✳✳✳✳

out of the wardrobe when you need that extra burst of confidence? Taking notice of what makes a fabric or garment special to you can become a personal tool that will help you focus on your spell craft.

For any exercises that involve helping you feel better about yourself, it may be useful to have something that acts like a magical robe. See if you can find, or better still make, your own magical robe. For those of you who sew, your magical robe could be anything from a bathrobe to an oversized dress to a theatrical cape with a hood.

You can incorporate beads, tassels, and secret pockets into your own design or a store-bought pattern. It is an excellent gift for yourself.

It is important that your magical robe is comfortable and fairly loose. Try to have your robe made from natural fiber such as silk, cotton, linen, wool, flax, or hemp. These fabrics allow your skin to breathe. Be generous with the quantity of cloth you use—it's important that you feel well and truly enfolded in the fabric, feeling it caress your skin.

Keep this garment only for special occasions: when you are spell casting or doing any of the exercises in this book.

SPELL CRAFT TIP

Sharp objects are not your friend

Never give a knife or a pair of scissors as a gift unless the recipient of the gift gives you a coin. Knives and scissors used to be thought to be able to cut the cord of friendship.

Stones

Like candles, precious and semiprecious stones also have magical vibrations that correspond to our emotions and desires. Precious stones include diamonds, rubies, and sapphires. Semiprecious stones include moonstones and amethysts. There are many semiprecious stones that are effective for spells.

If you are looking for a stone to help power your spell, a great way of finding the right stone for your purpose is to visit your favorite stone shop and pick up the first rock you see while thinking about your spell. Your intuition will often help you find

the right stone. If no stone makes its presence felt, then you might consider not using a stone for your spell.

When you collect your stones, cleanse them with salt water or in a stream—this will remove any negative vibrations they have. If you enjoy using stones and seem to have a few of them about, store them in a special box or basket, preferably lined with

STONE	MAGICAL PROPERTIES
agate	improves energy
amber	encourages good fortune
amethyst	improves a sense of your true beauty
aquamarine	strengthens inspiration
bloodstone	relieves depression
garnet	deepens friendships
jade	attracts wealth
jasper	protects against nightmares
lapis lazuli	relieves trauma
malachite	improves a sense of health
moonstone	attracts friendships and increases emotional strength
obsidian (black)	releases old negative feelings
obsidian (green)	protects against difficult people
pearl	releases anger
tourmaline	wins friends
turquoise	protects against negative actions

natural material (cotton, silk, flax, or hemp) to keep them safe. Place a list of your stones and any useful information about them in the box.

Stones are frequently useful in protection spells. They are also often used in charm bags—you carry the stone with you, letting it attract your wish to you constantly. If you were making a charm bag for a friendship spell, for example, it might contain a heart-shaped piece of rose quartz; if you were doing one for a money spell, it might contain a green stone, such as a piece of jade.

Choose the type of stone you wish to use from the table opposite. If you are still not sure about what stone to use, choose a piece of clear quartz crystal. This stone is very conducive to transmitting any type of magical purpose.

SPELL CRAFT TIP
Taking the energy of the seasons into account

When you are planning to cast a particular spell, remember what season you are in. Each season has its own energy, and this energy can enhance or counteract the power you generate for your spell. Use spring energy to cast new love spells; the heat of summer to power a protection spell; fall for money investment spells; and winter for spells asking for guidance.

Other natural ingredients

The wood and leaves of a tree, as well as flowers, can be very useful for a number of different types of spells. When using pieces of wood for your spells, it is best if you have found your wood already separated from the tree, like a branch blown off a tree by high winds or broken by a lightning strike. Do not break a branch, bark, or leaf off a tree. If you do, you will find that your spell will not be as effective as when using an already detached piece from a tree.

Small blocks or strips of wood that you can get from a hardware store, such as pine or balsa, can also be used for spells. Pine can be used for healing spells. For example, you can write the name of the person to whom you wish to send healing energies on a thin sliver of pine board. You may wish to draw happy images around the

person's name symbolizing comfort and pleasure. Balsa is useful for sending all sorts of psychic energy, so you can use this wood in protection charms.

For advanced spell craft, magical wands that help focus psychic energy can be made from certain trees. Traditionally, ash is the best wood for a magical wand. However, in simpler types of spells, a piece of wood can be included in a charm bag

TYPE OF WOOD	MAGICAL USE
ash	protects against negative energies
balsa	enhances protection spells
birch	heightens psychic energy
cedar	attracts money
elm	aids communication
holly	improves friendships
mistletoe	protects against negative energy
oak	attracts good luck
pine	enhances healing spells
rowan	attracts creativity
willow	aids all forms of healing

TYPE OF FLOWER	MAGICAL USE
cornflower	abundance, fertility
jasmine	sensual love
lavender	unresolved guilt
red rose	passionate love
sunflower	strength, courage, balancing self-esteem
tulip	mends bonds
violets	comfort in times of sorrow
water lily	love, calm

or simply carried in your pocket or wallet to attract a certain form of energy. See the table opposite for the magical use of various types of wood. The leaves of some of these trees can also be used in your spells. For example, the leaf of an ash tree on your bicycle or in your car can protect you against accidents. Place a leaf of the dogwood tree in your diary to keep it safe from prying eyes.

Flower magic is very sensitive and delicate, because cut flowers have a fairly short life span. It is a magic that is developed according to your own reactions to a flower's scent. Choose the flowers that mean the most to you. Maybe they remind you of a particular time or state of mind. Become familiar with those flowers and study their vibrations and what they mean to you. It is a very personal magic. Some of the traditional meanings for flowers are listed in the table above. Feel free to make your own chart.

TRADITIONAL SPELL

If you find the leaf of an elm, store it until you have a problem that is worrying you. Pierce the leaf three times with a pin, then put it under your pillow—you will dream the solution to your problem.

AMULETS AND SPELLS

Amulets are generally used to give the wearer protection against a multitude of disasters. Amulets can come in the form of a whole range of crafted objects, such as the symbol of a cross, the Star of David (six-pointed star), the pentagram (a five-pointed star), the Egyptian ankh ☥ , or a symbol in the shape of an eye.

Amulets can also be herbs, nuts, semiprecious stones, and other naturally occurring items, and may even be a specific part of an animal, bird, or reptile. If a person fears being attacked by a snake, a lion, or some other beast, they would wear some representation of that animal as a protection against being hurt by that creature. In traditional societies, hunters would go off to hunt wearing the skins, claws, or incisors of the animals they seek to capture, in order to avoid being attacked first.

Amulets are often worn as a piece of jewelry—a pendant or a ring, usually—or carried in a person's left-hand pocket or in the lining of a jacket or hat. The left-hand side represents the intuitive side of one's personality.

Traditionally, dark-colored stones and gems (such as carnelian and jet) have protective qualities, particularly if they are set in silver. Silver is a metal that corresponds with the energy of the moon, imbuing the wearer with psychic protection. Stones that have a naturally occurring hole (sometimes known as "holey stones," "hag stones" or "spirit stones") have been used for centuries as protection—they used to be hung near a sleeping person's head to protect against nightmares. Flint also has strong protective energies; when it is fashioned into a knife and hung over the threshold of a house, it protects the home from harm. Herbs such as basil are planted near a home to give it protection against misfortune and ill health. Other herbs of protection include dill, fennel, rosemary, and garlic. These herbs can be hung above all the openings of the house to the outside world to ensure protection against any negative energy that is inadvertently or deliberately directed at you.

HOW TO MAKE AN AMULET

Amulets were often used in necklaces to provide permanent protection against unfriendly supernatural forces and the major fears of life—death, poverty, and ill health. Collect the ingredients listed below to make an "all-purpose" amulet in the form of a bag that can be worn around your neck.

What do I need?

- A piece of red agate
- A piece of lapis lazuli
- A pinch of dried sage
- A silver or silver-colored ankh
- A piece of parchment paper or parchment-like paper (preferably 2 in. wide—though the precise length is not important)

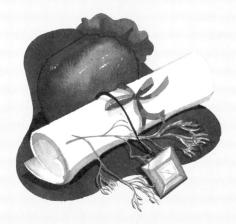

- A black marker pen
- A length of red string or ribbon (to bind around the piece of paper once it is rolled into a tight scroll)
- A red drawstring silk bag big enough to hold the above ingredients
- A black leather thong (long enough to hang around your neck)

When should I do this spell?

During the phase of the new moon

What should I do?

Place all the ingredients except the paper, pen, and string or ribbon in the bag. Agate is included because it symbolizes longevity; it has also been used as an amulet by itself to purify the blood and to soothe fevers. Lapis lazuli has been used because it aids in psychic protection. Sage is renowned for its association with longevity, and the Egyptian ankh is an ancient symbol of life.

Write the following words on the piece of paper:

Life, Prosperity, Health

Roll the paper into a tight scroll and tie the string or ribbon to secure the paper cylinder. Place it in the bag with the other ingredients. Pull the drawstring closed and tie the leather thong around the bag. Tie the ends of the thong and hang this powerful amulet around your neck. In Egyptian magic, many amulets were worn around the neck, as this area was seen to be vulnerable.

ANTI-SPELLS

SEE ALSO **PROTECTION AND SPELLS** ON PAGES 150–153.

Anti-spells are a form of spell that protects you against a specific problem, whether it be a school bully or feelings of envy or hurt. Here are a number of anti-spells for you to try.

ANTI-BULLY SPELL

School bullies are a fact of life, whether you are ten years old or a university student. The following spell to protect yourself against school bullies is directed at stopping their actions from hurting you—the spells in this book are not designed to manipulate other people.

What do I need?

• White liquid paper or a white marker pen
• A circle of black cardboard measuring 1 in. in diameter (as many as there are bullies against whom you seek protection)
• A white pencil case, either commercially bought or one that you make specially for this spell

When should I do this spell?

During the phase of the full moon

What should I do?

Using the white liquid paper or a white marker pen, write the following words on the black cardboard:

No bully will see me

On the other side of the cardboard, draw the symbol, shown right, which is the Mayan symbol of zero. This symbol is also linked to the Egyptian magical talisman against the evil eye, which is in the shape of an eye. By combining the words and the symbol, you are saying that the bully will not see you, and that his or her actions will come to naught.

Put the cardboard in the pencil case and keep it in your bag. By placing the amulet in the pencil case and keeping the zipper shut, you are keeping your local bullies in the dark, so that their actions will not harm you.

ANTI-EMBARRASSMENT SPELL

Being deliberately or accidentally embarrassed in class or at work is a nasty experience; it is also one that can be guarded against to some extent. One of the best ways of avoiding embarrassment is to make sure that you do not allow yourself to be made to feel stupid.

If you are at school, you are there to learn, so don't let anyone make you feel stupid. If there is anything you don't understand, simply ask questions until you do understand. Chances are, most of the rest of your class are as confused as you are but are too scared to ask the questions.

The following spell gives you a sense of courage to not feel embarrassment.

What do I need?
- A needle
- A small copper disc
- A pinch of dried basil leaves
- A small wooden box, preferably made of oak
- A picture of a dolphin
- A blue ribbon (optional)

When should I do this spell?
During the phase of the full moon

What should I do?

With your needle, draw the runic cross (*left*) on the copper disc. This runic cross will help protect you against all negative energies and will shield you from embarrassment and other unhappy experiences in the classroom.

Place the inscribed disc and dried basil leaves in the box. Fold the picture of the dolphin so that it fits into the box. If the picture refuses to stay flat, tie a blue ribbon around it. The dolphin symbolizes happiness, intelligence, and the element of water, which helps cleanse and protect the emotions from hurt.

Bring the box into class and place it on your desk—in the left-hand corner, near your elbow—or keep it in your bag by your left elbow. In feng shui, this corner of your desk corresponds to the learning and knowledge gathering aspects of your life. This little box will help save you from criticism and embarrassment when you are trying to learn.

ANTI-FEAR SPELL

The following spell is very useful in helping you identify what your fears are and burning them out of existence. This spell also features the powerful cleansing and protective properties of sage.

What do I need?

- Up to 10 thin slivers of balsa wood
- A black marker pen
- A metal bowl half filled with sand or dirt
- A small packet of dried sage (or a smudge stick, if you can get one)
- Matches
- A glass of water

When should I do this spell?

During the phase of the waning moon

What should I do?

On each piece of balsa wood, write a single word that encapsulates your fears. Some of your words might be:

> *humiliation*
> *rejection,* or
> *unfriendliness.*

Sprinkle the dried sage over the top of the dirt in your metal bowl. If you have a smudge stick, light it and pass it around the bowl three times.

Stack your balsa wood pieces beside the bowl and have your matches and a glass of water nearby. Balsa wood is used in this spell because it resonates and strengthens your psychic abilities.

Burn the pieces of wood, one by one, in your bowl, watching the smoke disappear into the air and visualizing that fear being removed from your psyche. When you have burned each fear, drink the glass of water; this symbolizes the cleansing of these fears from your physical system as well.

ANTI-GOSSIP SPELL

The following spell will give you a chance to get some respite from malicious and hurtful gossip. The spell is based on the simple but effective cleansing properties of soap. If you want to add a further calming element to the spell, use soap that has a lavender scent.

What do I need?

- A bamboo stick (or a small section of a willow branch)

- A bar of lavender-scented soap made from natural ingredients, if possible (you can get by with a bar of ordinary, natural soap)
- A few sprigs of lavender
- A white towel
- A silver-colored bowl of warm water

When should I do this spell?

During the phase of the full moon

What should I do?

With your bamboo stick, inscribe the topic of the gossip (one or a few words only) on the bar of soap. Don't press too deeply into the surface. The topic could be anything from accusations that you cheated on a test to allegations that you are in love with your boss.

Go outside and bathe the inscribed bar of soap in moonlight. Bring the lavender, towel, and bowl of water with you. Imagine that the moonlight is cleansing the hurt of the gossip from the energy around you. Imagine that the main perpetrators of the gossip are losing interest and finding better ways to spend their time. Feel that the gossip will not stick to you.

When you feel ready, rub the lavender into the soap, if you couldn't get lavender-scented soap. This action will help calm the effects of the gossip on you and on the people around you.

Using the soap, wash your hands in the bowl until the inscription has disappeared. Imagine that the bowl of water is the moon, and that she is removing and cleansing all the nasty influences around you. Pour the water into the ground, letting the Earth absorb the negativity, then use the towel to dry your hands.

The spell is now done. If your hands still feel a bit sudsy, go inside and wash your hands again, as you rinse the bowl.

ANTI-INJURY SPELL

This spell is focused on helping you avoid injury during a game. It will take a full week to construct a talisman, and you will need to carry the talisman with you into your matches. The talisman will use astrological symbols that invoke the energy of the planets that have, over many centuries, been believed to correspond to different parts of the body.

What do I need?

- A flat piece of oak, preferably circular and measuring 2 in. in diameter
- A drill with a small drill bit
- A leather thong (long enough to hang around your neck)
- A small, black drawstring bag (optional)
- A black marker pen

When should I do this spell?

Over the week before the game, ending on the morning of the game

What should I do?

The energy of the oak tree corresponds to strength and protection. Drill a hole near the top of the oak medallion and thread through it a thong that is long enough for you to be able to wear the medallion under your clothes. If you'd rather not have anything around your neck during the game (or you are not allowed to), put the finished talisman into the small black bag and carry it in your pocket.

Draw the following symbols around the edge of the oak medallion either at 1 P.M. or 8 P.M.:

⊙ SUNDAY (symbol of the Sun, protecting the sides and upper back)

☾ MONDAY (symbol of the Moon, protecting the stomach and chest)

♂ TUESDAY (symbol of Mars, protecting against cuts and burns)

☿ WEDNESDAY (symbol of Mercury, protecting arms and solar plexus)

♃ THURSDAY (symbol of Jupiter, protecting thighs and hamstrings)

♀ FRIDAY (symbol of Venus, protecting throat and lower back)

♄ SATURDAY (symbol of Saturn, protecting knees, teeth, and bones)

ANTI-MISFORTUNE SPELL

Misfortune is a wide term—it encompasses anything from mere inconvenience to life-threatening circumstances. The actions required to cast a protection spell are usually accompanied by a visualization of a shield that surrounds you and has the ability to deflect any negative energy.

What do I need?
• Five stones, each with a hole in the center
• Five gold-colored coins, each with a hole in the center
• Five lengths of red ribbon

When should I do this spell?
During the phase of the waning moon

What should I do?
Sit in a quiet area of your home where you will not be disturbed. When you feel ready, visualize building, stone by stone, a strong fortress around you. Feel the imagined weight of the stones as you put them on top of each other.

Stone is a symbol of the element of Earth, and can help you when you are casting spells against misfortune. As you visualize building your structure, imagine placing a gold coin between the stone blocks every so often. In some folk traditions, placing coins along the beams of a building or within the stones is considered essential to ward off evil. Build the walls as high as you like and feel them protecting you against all negativity.

Now tie a stone and a coin together with a length of red ribbon. Make four more bundles of stones and coins, imagining that they come from your enchanted fortress. Allow the image of the fortress to fade, but retain the sense of strength and protection it gave you. To end the spell, hang a bundle of stone, coin, and ribbon over each of the main openings of your home to the world—your front and back doors and the three largest windows, perhaps. As you hang each bundle up securely, say the following words:

Protect my body, my home, and my loved ones
From misfortune and harm.

ANTI-NIGHTMARE SPELL

In Native American traditions, it was thought that evil spirits caused nightmares. The Native Americans created the dream catcher—a woven web within a wooden circle with a piece of string and a feather attached—and would hang it over the bed of an adult or infant suffering nightmares. The dream catcher's purpose is to entangle the evil and allow only the good dreams to filter through the web and down the string to the person sleeping below. The following spell is based on the concept of a dream catcher, but uses instead a ready-made willow garland, which can be purchased at many arts and craft stores.

What do I need?
- A willow garland in a shape reminiscent of a crescent moon
- Three lengths of ribbon—blue, purple, and white—each the width of your bed
- One circular piece of silver cardboard
- A black permanent marker pen
- Two pieces of silver cardboard shaped like the crescent moon
- A piece of turquoise
- A piece of amethyst
- A piece of moonstone
- Some dried bunches of chamomile flowers or lavender

When should I do this spell?
During the phase of the waning moon

What should I do?
Purchase or make your willow garland. Before using it in the spell, take the garland outside and let it spend one night under the light of the moon. Thread the three lengths of ribbon at random through the garland.

On a magical level, your sleep is governed by the psychic power of the moon. To invoke the positive protection of the moon, write the following words on the back of the full moon (circular) piece of silver cardboard:

Goddess Moon,

Give me rest and sweet dreams.

Decorate the garland with the full moon and the other cardboard shapes, stones, and dried chamomile or lavender flowers. Hang the garland over your pillow.

ANTI-THEFT SPELL

Burglar alarms, strong locks, automatic outdoor lights, watchdogs, and other precautions must always be considered when you are seeking to protect your home against burglary. However, extra protection can be given by spells that are designed to distract a burglar from choosing your home to rob, or to disperse negative energy already aimed at your home. The following spell is based on a feng shui technique.

What do I need?
• A bowl of slightly salty water
• Faceted crystals
• A bunch of fennel or dill
• White ribbon

When should I do this spell?
During the phase of the full moon

What should I do?
As the moon rises in the evening, walk around your house in a counterclockwise direction, sprinkling salted water around the perimeter. If you live in an apartment, walk around the inside perimeter of your space. The salt purifies and cleanses the space around you.

As you are walking, take note of the view outside your windows and external doors. Are there are any poles, rooflines, straight paths, or oncoming traffic flows directly facing these windows or doors?

These elements in your environment send a "poison energy" straight toward your windows and doors; if your home is not shielded, they will create negative energy that can attract burglars.

To shield your home, hang a clear quartz crystal in each window and above each door affected by the poison energy. Hang a small bunch of fennel or dill tied with white ribbon with each crystal.

AROMATHERAPY AND SPELLS

The pure essential oils extracted from flowers and herbs can be effective magical tools. Below is a list of recipes for use in your oil burner. Using these can create an atmosphere suited to spells, meditations, and visualizations.

PROTECTION BLEND

Use during protection spells, rituals, and when feeling threatened.
* One part (e.g. 2 drops) cedarwood, two parts (e.g. 4 drops) sandalwood, and one half part (e.g. 1 drop) clove
* Add four peppercorns to the water bowl or a few threads of a spider's web

PSYCHIC BLEND

Use before and during spiritual and psychic work.
* One part (e.g. 2 drops) frankincense and one part (e.g. 2 drops) sandalwood
* Add a few saffron threads to the water bowl

PROSPERITY BLEND

Use during prosperity spells or to draw wealth to the home.
* One part (e.g. 2 drops) peppermint, one part (e.g. 2 drops) basil, and one half part (e.g. 1 drop) bergamot
* Add five small coins to the water bowl

LUCK AND SUCCESS BLEND

Use during spells to draw the energies of luck and success.
* One quarter part (e.g. half a drop) citronella, two parts lemongrass (e.g. 4 drops), and one half part (e.g. 1 drop) cinnamon
* Add a small cinnamon quill to the water bowl

PURIFYING BLEND

Use during spells or after an unhappy, unpleasant experience in the home. Also excellent for use when moving into a new home.

• One part (e.g. 2 drops) sage, one part (e.g. 2 drops) rosemary, and one half part (e.g. 1 drop) clove
• Add a pinch of salt to the water bowl

GROUNDING BLEND

Use when feeling unsettled, depressed, or fearful.

• One part (e.g. 3 drops) vetiver and one part (e.g. 3 drops) oak moss or pine
• Add a pinch of earth or a hematite crystal to the water bowl

SLUMBER BLEND

Use before sleep and to inspire prophetic dreams.

• One part (e.g. 3 drops) marjoram or oregano and one part (e.g. 3 drops) lavender
• Add a moonstone crystal to the water bowl

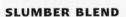

AN AROMATHERAPY LOVE PHILTER

The following heady blend of luscious essential oils is best burned in an aromatherapy oil burner in a room where lovers are to meet. The blend is believed to be pleasing to the spirits of love, and may inspire lovers to enhance their lovemaking. The recipe is based on a Caribbean love oil worn by young girls who wish to attract a lover.

What do I need?

• Two drops of essential oil of patchouli
• Two drops of essential oil of orange
• Two drops of essential oil of cinnamon
• A hint of essential oil of clove
• An oil burner
• A tea light
• Matches
• Two drops of essential oil of vetiver (optional)
• Three teaspoons of pure virgin olive oil in a small bottle (optional)
• Thirteen small red candles (optional)

When should I do this spell?

Anytime

What should I do?

Combine the essential oils in the oil burner and burn them while reciting the following words:

Bring to me a lover true

If you wish to wear this blend of essential oils on your skin as a love perfume, add the specified number of drops of each to 3 teaspoons of pure virgin olive oil and shake well.

This love formula may be modified slightly and turned into a potent attraction oil with the addition of two drops of essential oil of vetiver. To draw a person near and fill them with longing, place a little of this modified potion on each of 13 small red candles and recite the name of the desired person 169 times over the candles. The magic should grow stronger with each recitation. When the energy has reached its peak, at the final recitation, blow the candles out to ground the magic.

ATTRACTION SPELLS

ATTRACTING EMPLOYMENT SPELL

This spell is designed to attract employment that suits you, as opposed to getting just any job; you can also factor into the spell how much money you wish to make per year from the new job. This spell involves making a special talisman (see also "Talismans and Spells" on pages 168–170). This talisman represents the energy of Mars, a useful celestial energy to invoke for this type of spell (see also "Celestial Bodies and Spells" on pages 46–47).

What do I need?

- A flat piece of cedar wood (approximately 2 in. square or round)
- A silver marker pen
- Red cloth made from natural fiber

When should I do this spell?

On a Tuesday

What should I do?

On the wood, use your marker pen to draw the Mars number square (*right*).

11	24	7	20	3
4	12	25	8	16
17	5	13	21	9
10	18	1	14	22
23	6	19	2	15

As cedar is a soft wood, it is relatively easy to mark the lines and numbers. If you have difficulty drawing the Mars square on your wood, photocopy the square from this book (or draw it on paper) and paste it onto the wood, using your silver marker to reinforce the lines. Wrap the talisman in the red cloth and keep it with you at all times until you get a job.

ATTRACTING FRIENDLY, HELPFUL PEOPLE

You can use some of the principles of feng shui to create a spell that will attract friendly or helpful people to you. The spell requires you to make an amulet and then position a wind chime or hand bell in a strategic position in your bedroom and/or on your study table.

What do I need?
• Pliers
• A length of thin copper wire
• A small handful of terra-cotta clay
• A small brown drawstring bag
• A set of wind chimes and/or a hand bell

When should I do this spell?
Two nights before starting at a new school, college, or job

What should I do?
Face north and use your pliers to fashion the copper wire into a "P" shape. This shape is the "wungo" rune, which corresponds to harmony and friendship. Shape your terra-cotta into a flat circle and press the metal "P" into the clay. Let the clay dry. When it is dry, put the amulet in the drawstring bag and place it in your bag or in your right jacket pocket. On the evening before your first day, stand in the doorway into your bedroom, then move to the corner to your right—hang the wind chimes in that corner of your bedroom. If you have a study desk at home, also place a hand bell on the bottom right-hand corner of your desk, nearest your right elbow as you are sitting at your desk.

SPELL CRAFT TIP

An aromatherapy blend to attract spiritual aid

In an oil burner, combine one part (e.g. 3 drops) violet, hyacinth, or narcissus and one part (e.g. 3 drops) chamomile or lavender oil. Add a piece of angelica, lotus root, or a couple of white rose petals to the water bowl to enhance the potion.

ATTRACTING MONEY FOR A PARTICULAR PURPOSE SPELL
The following spell features candle magic, which is a powerful way of getting what you want. The green candle resonates with energy of growth and nurture: green corresponds with the Earth element, and green objects are often used in money and prosperity spells (*see also* "Money Spells" on pages 135–136 and "Prosperity Spells" on pages 148–150).

This spell also features a picture. The picture is usually placed underneath the candleholder—it directs the energy specifically to what you want to buy. Although the picture is only representative of your wish, try to find an image that includes as many details of your wish as possible. You may draw the image.

What do I need?

- Picture of what you want to buy
- Stable wooden candleholder
- Green candle
- Matches

When should I do this spell?
On a Thursday

What should I do?
Find a safe place where you can leave your candle to burn without damaging anything. Lie the picture on a stable, nonflammable surface and put the candleholder on top of it.

Place the candle in the candleholder. Light the candle. Take a few moments to stare into the flame. Sit comfortably and concentrate

---

SPELL CRAFT TIP

Other aromatherapy love potions

To draw a lover into one's life or to enhance an existing relationship, place the following essential oils in your oil burner: one part (e.g. 2 drops) rose geranium, one half part (e.g. 1 drop) lavender and one part (e.g. 2 drops) gardenia or ylang ylang. Add a few rose or geranium petals to the water bowl. Another potion, perfect for use in the bedroom or during love spells, is one part (e.g. 2 drops) cinnamon, one quarter part (e.g. half a drop) clove, two parts (e.g. 4 drops) orange and one part (e.g. 2 drops) patchouli. Add a piece of fresh ginger to the water bowl.

on your breathing. Breathe in for a count of four and out for a count of four.

When you feel ready, close your eyes and visualize what you want. Construct the image in your mind in every detail, seeing it in the position of your "third eye" (in the middle of your forehead).

Leave the candle to burn down to the end.

ATTRACTING LOVE SPELL

This spell is designed to help you attract love, in all its forms, into your life. This spell will allow you to feel that you are worthy of love. It will give you the power to attract all sorts of love—the love of your family, friends, coworkers, in fact, everyone you come into contact with (*see also* "Love and Spells" on pages 117–122, the "Love Magnet Spell" on page 123, the "Love Powder Spell" on page 124, and "True Love Spells" on pages 172–173).

What do I need?
- A plain white sheet of paper
- Two pens, one black and one red
- Two pink roses
- A glass jar
- Scissors
- A bowl of water

When should I do this spell?
Anytime you feel unloved and alone

What should I do?
Cut the sheet of paper in half.
Using the red pen, write down all the things that you feel make you lovable on one of the sheets.

On the other sheet, with the black pen, write all the things you can think of that you feel make you unlovable.

Place the positive sheet near a window, and put the two roses in the glass jar on top of it. This will start the spell of attraction.

Place the negative sheet in the bowl of water. Watch the paper disintegrate and the ink run until the writing is no longer legible. Throw out the soggy sheet.

Leave the positive sheet and jar in place for the full cycle of the moon, replacing the flowers with fresh ones whenever they start to droop.

B

BELONGINGS PROTECTION SPELLS

There are many ways to protect your belongings, apart from the
common sense strategies of locking them out of harm's way and
keeping an eye on them. Spells help guard your possessions in
circumstances beyond your control, and when you become less than
vigilant because of other distractions. The following spell focuses on
a feng shui way of dispersing negative energy so that a thief will not
be attracted to the belongings you take with you when you are away
from home.

What do I need?

• A red tassel
• A wooden or plastic fan
• Glue
• Two cabochons of carnelian or garnet (a cabochon is a method of
  cutting the stone so that it is flat on one side and slightly
  rounded or domed on the other side)

When should I do this spell?

On the last full moon before your date of departure

What should I do?

Attach the red tassel to the wire connecting the sticks of the fan
together and glue the two cabochons (by the flat sides) to the
outside faces of the two end sticks of the fan.

Open up the fan and place it on top of your belongings in your
suitcase or traveling bag. Do not let the sticks of the fan break. It is
important that when you open your suitcase at your destination,
the fan is the first thing you see. If the sticks of the fan are broken
when you arrive, replace the fan with a new one
and repeat the spell.

In feng shui, the display of a fan is
believed to be enough to disperse any
negative energy, such as the attention
of a thief. In Western magic, the fan is a
symbol of authority and power.

PROTECTING AGAINST THE THEFT OF A VALUED POSSESSION SPELL

Many spells use images to help protect a valued possession. For the following spell, you need to take a photograph of the object you wish to protect and anchor it to the place where it belongs.

What do I need?
- A silver marker pen
- A piece of white cardboard the same size as the photograph
- Glue
- A photograph of the valued possession
- A heavy river stone or a heavy earthenware pot

When should I do this spell?
During the phase of the full moon

What should I do?

With your silver pen, draw the image on the left, called an algiz or rune of protection, onto the piece of cardboard. Then glue the piece of cardboard onto the image of the valued possession. This symbolically screens the object from sight.

Place the image on the floor in the room where the object is kept, just inside the doorway, and place the stone or pot over the combined photograph and protective image. This placement means that the piece is protected, and is anchored to stay within the energy of the room.

BIG DATE SPELL

As you prepare for an important date, consider enhancing your attractiveness not only by choosing your clothes and makeup carefully, but also by releasing your energy and letting your inner beauty glow brightly.

Do the following meditation based on the seven energy centers running through your body, called chakras. This meditation is also useful for getting rid of pre-date jitters—it will help you feel strong and balanced throughout your date, giving you a sense of confidence and poise.

What do I need?
- Just a quiet place where you will not be interrupted

When should I do this spell?
For three nights before your date
What should I do?
Sit in a quiet place on the floor or on the
ground. Sit on a soft cushion if the surface is
too hard. Imagine energy flowing from the
Earth through to the base of your spine and
"lighting up" a red glow at that point.

Imagine the energy flowing up your spine
through each chakra and feel each area being
"lit" up with its appropriate color. The colors
of the chakra energy centers correspond to
the following seven colors of the rainbow:

CHAKRA POSITION	CORRESPONDING COLOR
base of the spine	red
sacrum (just below the navel)	orange
solar plexus	yellow
heart	green
throat	blue
middle of the forehead (the "Third Eye")	indigo
top of the head	violet

Once the energy reaches the top of your head, allow it to flow back
to the ground. Imagine the energy looping back up your spine,
feeding your body with a continuous flow of vitality and strength.
Keep this feeling with you when you go on your date. When you get
back home, imagine reversing the flow of the energy, out of your
body and into the ground, and allow the light in the chakras to dim.

BRINGING BACK A LOVER SPELL

The southern American state of Louisiana conjures up images of
stately mansions surrounded by ancient trees fringed with Spanish
moss. It is also a place where powerful magic has been woven for
centuries. The warm, moist climate of the American South is
believed to be highly conducive to magical vibrations. Some
psychics and magicians believe that the spells cast and created there

are among the most potent on Earth. The spiritual heartland of southern-style magic is Africa, and the spells of the South often have a distinctly African flavor.

The following spell is remarkably simple: it uses a few basic ingredients, plus a good deal of creative visualization.

What do I need?
• Five red candles
• A small pot of honey
• A sprinkling of powdered cinnamon
• A sprinkling of sugar
• A photograph of your lover
• Matches
• A piece of red cloth big enough to wrap around the photograph

When should I do this spell?
During the phase of the waxing moon

What should I do?
In Louisiana, five red candles burned before the photograph of a missing loved one are thought to draw him or her back to you.

Smear each candle with honey and dust each with cinnamon powder and sugar, then arrange the candles in a circle around the photograph and light them. Call the name of your lover 109 times as the candles burn and visualize him or her returning to you with an open heart and open arms.

Leave the candles to burn away to nothing. Wrap the photograph in the cloth and place it underneath your bed.

SPELL CRAFT TIP

Honey come back to me

Another similar spell involves piercing a photograph of your loved one with 30 brand-new fishing hooks and putting it in a jar of honey mixed with perfume. Place the jar within the circle of five red candles.

C

CALMING ARGUMENTS SPELLS

CLEARING SPACE AFTER AN ARGUMENT

Arguments can create a sense of heaviness and dissatisfaction in a room, even a whole house. After a particularly fierce argument, tensions often remain so thickly in the air that we feel the atmosphere could be cut with a knife. These tensions can literally stop the flow of energy through your home. It is important to clear the air after an argument so that beneficial energy can flow in and help you resolve the crisis.

What do I need?

• Two heavy sticks that make a sharp sound when struck together
• A melodious hand bell or Tibetan bells
• A stick of frankincense incense
• Matches

When should I do this spell?

As soon after the argument as possible

What should I do?

Walk through the house, or just go directly to the affected room. Breathe deeply and slowly and be conscious of the Earth's energy under your feet. Wear a protective amulet or talisman while you go through the scene of the argument (*see* "Amulets and Spells" on pages 24–25 or "Talismans and Spells" on pages 168–170).

Feel the energy of the affected room. If you feel that the colors of the room seem duller, or that your footsteps seem more muted than usual, take the two sticks to each corner of the room and hit them together sharply.

Put the sticks down and pick up the bell or bells. Walk counter-clockwise around the room while ringing the bell(s) at regular intervals—every four steps, for example.

When you feel ready, light the stick of frankincense incense and leave it to burn out in the middle of the room. Frankincense is a powerful protector against strong negative energies.

RESOLVING ARGUMENTS SPELLS

Even in the closest friendship or in the tightest group, arguments flare up. Try the following spell to resolve your differences.

What do I need?

- A silver bowl full of water (the bowl should be big enough for two people to hold easily)
- A small bowl of salt
- A stick of sandalwood incense
- Matches
- A mauve, light blue, or pink candle

When should I do this spell?

As soon as possible after the anger has died down

What should I do?

Sit opposite but close to your friend, with the bowl of water and other items between you. Each of you put a pinch of salt into the bowl, saying:

By the powers of Earth, we are united.

Light the incense, and each of you blow some incense smoke over the bowl, saying:

By the powers of Air, we are connected.

Light the candle, and each of you pass the bowl over the candle flame, saying:

By the powers of Fire, our [anger/pain/hurt/fear] is transformed.

The two of you hold the bowl up together, saying:

By the powers of Water, our friendship is cleansed.

As you hold the bowl together, think of the recent argument, misunderstanding, or hurt, remembering the negative feelings you experienced. Visualize these feelings as a murky substance that is now flowing through your arms and hands and into the bowl. When you are both ready, take the bowl and empty it, either in a running stream or down the drain in the bathroom.

CELESTIAL BODIES AND SPELLS

The position of the celestial bodies in the sky has for many centuries governed spell-casting practices. Traditionally, seven heavenly bodies have been used for spell casting—the sun, the moon, Mercury, Venus, Mars, Jupiter, and Saturn (the three outer planets are relatively recent discoveries).

Each celestial body is believed to have its own type of energy, and each is therefore useful for powering particular types of spells. To link into a particular celestial body's energy, a spell incorporates ingredients or symbols that represented that celestial body. The spell should be performed on the day of the week associated with the celestial body.

On Sunday, spells associated with the sun, such as those for wealth, fortune, and friendships, are performed. Spells associated with the moon, such as those for reconciliation and the strengthening of psychic abilities, are performed on Monday.

Tuesday, the day ruled by Mars, is a good day to perform spells to increase courage and attract protection. Mercury corresponds to Wednesday, a day when spells for eloquence, success in business partnerships, and protection against theft should be performed.

On Thursday, spells associated with Jupiter, such as those for the acquisition of money, material possessions, new friendships, and good health, are performed. Spells associated with Venus, such as

CELESTIAL BODY	COLOR	METAL	STONES OR RESINS
Sun	yellow, gold	gold	amber, carnelian, topaz, tiger's eye
Moon	white, silver	silver	moonstone, pearl, mother of pearl, clear quartz crystal
Mercury	yellow	mercury, quicksilver	agate, jasper, mica, aventurine
Venus	green	copper malachite	emerald, jade, lapis lazuli
Mars	red	iron	bloodstone, garnet, lava, ruby
Jupiter	purple	tin	amethyst
Saturn	brown, black	lead	hematite, jet, obsidian, onyx

love spells, are cast on Friday, and spells for business success, luck, and the acquisition of learning are performed on Saturday, as they correspond to the energy of Saturn.

The moon plays another role in determining when to perform particular spells. This celestial body governs all psychic work, and experienced spell casters are careful to perform certain spells during appropriate phases of the moon (new moon, waxing, full, waning, or dark moon). The most powerful time to perform spells is at full moon.

Use the table opposite as a guide to the type of energies, in terms of colors, metals, and stones, that are associated with the traditional seven celestial bodies (see also the tables on corresponding spells on page 14, herbs on page 102, and celestial energy on page 168).

A SPECIAL COSMIC SPELL FOR HELP

What do I need?

• A gold-colored disc for the sun
• A piece of moonstone for the moon
• Four almonds for Mercury
• A piece of copper for Venus
• A piece of dried ginger for Mars
• The letter "F" for Saturn
• The following symbol on a piece of deep blue fabric for Jupiter:

♃

• A silver drawstring bag

When should I do this spell?

Anytime you like

What should I do?

Collect all the ingredients, asking each celestial body to give you the help you need. Put all the items in the drawstring bag and carry the bag with you until you receive the help you need or are given guidance that will help you out of trouble.

CHARMS AND SPELLS

SEE ALSO **AMULETS AND SPELLS** ON PAGES 24–25.

Charms are magical words or chants used to ward off evil or
undesirable circumstances. A charm can also be a prayer. There
have been charms since ancient times, and they deal with many
contingencies, the most common being related to health and love.
There are many charms that have been handed down, with
variations, through generations. The following charm for being
shown your future lover was once very popular:

Good St. Thomas, do me right
And bring my love to me this night
That I do look him in the face
And in my arms may him embrace

Charms are often accompanied by ritualized actions, such as
spitting or wrapping onion peel in linen. Some of the charms that
have come down to us are hard to carry out because the actions

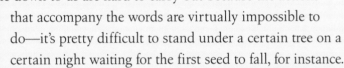

that accompany the words are virtually impossible to
do—it's pretty difficult to stand under a certain tree on a
certain night waiting for the first seed to fall, for instance.

Some charms are designed to be said while you are making
preparations for spell craft, particularly if you are gathering fresh
herbs for a healing spell. You can also make up your own charm—a
line or two of words—asking the herbs to release their most potent
energy to help heal your patient. If you can make the words rhyme,
the charm will be more powerful and, of course, easier to
remember.

Charms can be written down on parchment or wood and worn
around the neck in a decorative container, preferably with a secret
catch; they can also be incorporated into amulets—the word
"abracadabra," for example, is thought to have started out as part of
a cure for fever. Amulets with inscriptions are often called charms.

A POWERFUL GOOD LUCK CHARM

Traditionally, a charm was a magical phrase that was repeated to
help bring luck and protection. Today, however, a "lucky charm" can
be any object that has favorable associations for you. Try the
following spell to make a powerful lucky charm.

What do I need?

• An orange, violet, or green drawstring bag

- A yellow feather (not from a dead bird—find someone who has a pet canary)
- A semiprecious stone with which you identify
- An unshelled hazelnut
- A pinch of one of the following herbs—golden seal, angelica, yellow mustard seeds, St. John's Wort (hypericum), or nutmeg
- A dried chili bean
- A cowry shell
- Seven green candles
- Matches
- Incense (optional)

When should I do this spell?

During the phase of the full moon

What should I do?

Put the bag and the other spell ingredients in front of you, and place the seven candles in a semicircle around and behind them. You can also burn some incense while casting this spell. Light the candles, then pick up the bag and put the following items (in the order listed) into the bag, saying the following words:

Feather—By the power of Air
Chili bean—By the power of Fire
Cowry shell—By the power of Water
Stone—By the power of Earth
Hazelnut—By the power of Spirit
Herb—By all the powers of Nature.

Hold the bag tight and say, "And the power of my true will." Close the bag and say, "My life shall be blessed with good luck." The bag is now charged with objects symbolizing the elements, the spirit, nature, and your own true energy. Carry it with you wherever you go.

SPELL CRAFT TIP

A simple lucky stone charm

Aventurine, lodestone, and any L-shaped stones are said to attract good luck. If you manage to acquire one of these, wear it around your neck, carry it in your pocket or in put it into a small bag so that good luck will follow you every day!

CHILDREN AND SPELLS

Since ancient times, many simple actions have been devised to protect children from harm. In early human history, there was a fear that fairies or evil spirits would steal a child because he or she was so beautiful. In modern times, abduction by ill-intentioned people is still a major concern.

A number of traditions evolved to protect children, such as lining their pockets with salt. Salt was an early form of protection against impure thoughts and actions. In ancient times, Celtic parents deterred evil spirits by sewing an iron pin into a child's hat or piece of clothing. Iron has for centuries been considered an important protection against evil intentions and magic.

Horseshoes, which were traditionally made of iron, were considered excellent protection against evil spirits. If you fear your child being taken away in the night, or if you wish to implement a subtle form of making sure your child does not stray in the night, nail a horseshoe over the exterior sill of the child's bedroom window. The horseshoe's resemblance to the shape of the crescent moon was considered a particularly useful deterrent to nighttime spirits.

Some traditions were less wholesome—allowing a person who was thought to be cursed with the "evil eye" to spit on the child, for instance. It was thought that a person's eyes were capable of sending out magical messages that could manipulate or enslave the soul of a vulnerable child or an impressionable teenager or adult. This is the basis of the concept of the evil eye. (Spit, especially upon waking, was believed to be a powerful way of transmitting magical power or protection.) People who seemed to be always undergoing trauma and misfortune, or were lame, disfigured, or suffering from an

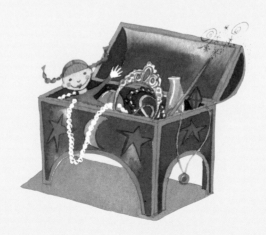

intellectual impediment, were often the sort of people thought to be cursed with the evil eye.

Children were often given an amuletic symbol to protect them against evil. The amulet either linked to their parents' religious beliefs or the power of nature.

So strong was this concept that, since ancient Egyptian times, people have worn pendants in the shape of an eye to protect themselves against the evil intentions of others. The Egyptian "Eye of Horus" is one of the most popular eye-shaped amulets; it is also believed to attract health and strength.

Sometimes an eye shape is drawn on a small mirror which is enclosed in a locket-style pendant—any evil intentions directed at the wearer are then reflected back to the person with the evil intentions. In some magical traditions, it is believed that the strength of the evil will be reflected back threefold.

SPELL CRAFT TIP

Birthstones and your child

Over the centuries, a number of different shapes and certain natural objects, such as herbs, crystals, and gems, have come to be thought of as lucky. These include stones that resonate with your birthday—your birthstone. Use the table below to find out your child's particular birthstone; it can be worn as protection.

SUN SIGN	YOUR BIRTHSTONES
Aries: March 20 to April 20	bloodstone, opal, diamond
Taurus: April 21 to May 21	amethyst, moss agate, sapphire
Gemini: May 22 to June 21	lapis lazuli, moonstone, emerald
Cancer: June 22 to July 22	carnelian, pearl, ruby
Leo: July 23 to August 23	amber, black onyx, peridot
Virgo: August 24 to September 23	jade, sardonyx, jasper
Libra: September 24 to October 23	chrysolite, coral, tourmaline
Scorpio: October 24 to November 23	malachite, topaz, aquamarine
Sagittarius: November 24 to December 21	turquoise, moonstone, topaz
Capricorn: December 22 to January 20	jet, garnet, ruby
Aquarius: January 21 to February 18	jade, amethyst, sapphire
Pisces: February 19 to March 20	opal, pearl, moonstone

SPECIAL PROTECTION SPELL TO KEEP CHILDREN SAFE

When your children are away at summer camp, or even just at school for the day, try the following spell to help them keep safe and to encourage them not to take too many risks.

What do I need?

• Your child's favorite toy

• A white ribbon

• A clear quartz crystal (a cluster or a piece as large as the palm of your hand)

When should I do this spell?

During the phase of the full moon

What should I do?

Tie the white ribbon around the hand of the toy, or some other part of the toy that can be tied easily. Do not tie the ribbon around the toy's neck if you are using a teddy bear or a favorite doll. Stuffed toys in particular pick up psychic energy from the child and can be used to symbolize the child.

As you make a knot in the white ribbon visualize the knot anchoring protective energy into the ribbon and the toy—imagine a glow of protective blue light encompassing the whole toy, then concentrate that energy into the knot.

Tie the other end of the white ribbon loosely around the crystal. This stone represents the stabilization of the protective energy you have created, and will encourage the energy to flow steadily and safely to your child.

**PLACING A NEWBORN UNDER
THE GUIDANCE AND PROTECTION OF THE UNIVERSE**

The following spell is a beautiful method of protecting a newborn baby as well as of calling the universal energies of love and guidance to lead the baby through the trials of life with strength and resolution.

What do I need?

• A bunch of sweet-smelling flowers that will dry over time, such as roses and lavender

• String to tie up the flowers

• A piece of white cloth big enough to wrap the dried flowers in

When should I do this spell?

On a Wednesday morning

What should I do?

Sit comfortably on the floor with the baby. Place the bunch of flowers beside the baby. Do not burn incense—it may alarm or irritate the child.

Close your eyes and visualize a stream of brilliant white light enshrouding you and the child. Take the child's hands in yours and recite the following:

Forces of pure white light, spirits of the Earth, of Fire, and Water and Air, be here with us and witness my pledge.

I dedicate this young life to the forces of purity, love, and truth. With peace and love I give over this child to the path of bliss and learning.

Take a flower from the bunch and hold it above the child while saying the following words:

Forces of love please place this child under your guidance and protection. May her/his path in this life be smooth and may all her/his lessons be learned with grace and strength.

Kiss the child and enjoy the moment. Use the string to hang the bunch of flowers somewhere to dry out. When they are dry, wrap them in the cloth and store them in a safe place. Sprinkle a few crushed petals from the dried flowers underneath the child's bed on each birthday to call the forces of love to the child's side.

CLARITY SPELLS

CLARITY SPELL: WHAT DO THEY WANT TO KNOW?

When you are taking an exam, it is very important to understand precisely what each question is asking, and clarity of mind may be difficult to achieve in an exam. Try the following spell during the height of the sun's powers (at noon) the day before your exam. The spell involves making an amulet, which you can take into the exam with you or leave on the left-hand corner of your desk (the corner nearest your left elbow) at home.

What do I need?

- A sheet of parchment paper
- A pinch of the following dried herbs:
  basil
  rosemary
  marjoram
  cinnamon
- Two drops of geranium
  essential oil
- A piece of tiger's eye
- A piece of clear quartz crystal
- A blue envelope
- Blue ribbon

When should I do this spell?

The day before your exam, at noon

What should I do?

Gather your ingredients together either outside or near a window where you can see the sun. Place the piece of paper on a table where the surface catches the sunlight and write the word "Clarity" in the middle of the sheet. Put a pinch of each herb on the sheet, covering the word. Sprinkle the two drops of oil over the herbs. Place the tiger's eye on the sheet, next to the pile of herbs.

Hold the crystal between the paper and the sun, so that the sunlight shines through it onto the herbs, and visualize the sun increasing the clarity that will be at your command when you sit down to take your exam. Now place the tiger's eye in the pocket of a piece of clothing that you are going to wear during the exam. Tiger's eye is an excellent stone for keeping your mind clear.

Fold the herbs into the paper, then tie the ribbon around the package and place it in the envelope. The envelope does not need to be near you in the exam; pack it into your school bag or briefcase or leave it on your study desk.

CLARITY SPELL: IS HE OR SHE WORTH THE EFFORT?

Sometimes we may be strongly attracted to someone who seems to be very charismatic, good-looking, exciting, or simply "cool." However, we sometimes discover, too late, that the person is not right for us. To avoid repeating this relationship pattern, do this clarity spell—it will help you clarify what your needs are within a relationship. You will then have a better chance of working out whether or not they are likely to be fulfilled with a particular person.

What do I need?

• A piece of paper
• A pen
• Two geranium flower petals or two drops of geranium essential oil
• Two pinches of the following dried herbs:
  basil leaves
  rosemary
  marjoram
  cinnamon
• A small clear quartz crystal
• A small blue fabric drawstring bag

When should I do this spell?

At noon on any day

What should I do?

First, write down on a piece of paper what you want in a relationship, starting with the really important things—for example, good communication, affection, friendship, fun, mutual respect, support, caring, and sharing. Then gather the spell ingredients.

Perform this spell outside, or next to a window where you can see the sun. At noon, place the two geranium petals in the middle of the piece of paper you've written on and sprinkle the herbs on top of the petals. If you are using geranium essential oil, sprinkle the herbs first, then pour the two drops of oil over the herbs. Hold the crystal between the paper and the sun, so that the sunlight shines through it onto the herbs. Imagine yourself clear and aware of the realities of your situation, and firmly say the following, three times:

> *O mighty Sun, at your greatest height*
> *All is shown in your clearest light.*
> *By my spell help me to see*
> *If he/she is really right for me.*

Fold the herbs and petals or oil into the paper and place the paper in the bag, with the crystal. Carry the bag in your pocket or around your neck as long as you feel you need clarification about your feelings for a particular person.

CONCENTRATION IMPROVING SPELLS

The following spell is very useful for helping you concentrate on your work or studies. The spell is based on a very important concept in magic, called grounding. By tapping into the power of the Earth, all unnecessary thoughts and actions seem to melt away and you are left free to focus on the job at hand.

What do I need?
• Two heavy stones (river stones or, preferably, ironstone)
• A black marker pen

When should I do this spell?
During the phase of the full moon or whenever you need to concentrate on a project, assignment, or your studies

What should I do?
If possible, go outside with your stones and pen. Stand on a patch of grass in a spot where you will not be disturbed. Place one stone on the ground and write on the stone what you want to concentrate on. For example, write the name of your assignment or the topic of your studies.

Stand behind that stone and hold the other stone in your hands and feel its weight anchoring you into the ground. Imagine your feet sinking into the ground and the energy of the Earth flowing up into your body. Feel this energy moving through you, and imagine all thoughts other than those concerning your desired focus for concentration draining away from you into the Earth.

When you feel ready, place the stone that is in your hands on top of the stone on the ground and push down, visualizing your heightened levels of concentration being anchored into the topic of your choice. Leave the stones in this position, if possible, and go back inside to do some serious work.

CONFIDENCE SPELL

This spell involves invoking the energy of a totem animal that symbolizes confidence to us—for example, any of the big cats, such as tigers, panthers, and lions, or birds, such as eagles, hawks, and owls. All these creatures have a detached quality in their interaction with strangers. They watch them, and are powerful in dealing with intruders within their space.

What do I need?

- A small, smooth, rounded river stone or one that you have found on the seashore
- Four drops of patchouli oil
- A red candle
- A stable candleholder
- A picture of the animal you wish to have as your confidence companion
- Matches

- A black marker pen

When should I do this spell?

Anytime

What should I do?

Choose a stone that you have found during your holidays or some other time when you were feeling happy and carefree. The stone should be small enough for you to carry in your pocket or bag. Wash the stone in running water and place it on the ground for two hours. Bring the stone inside.

Rub the patchouli oil onto your candle. Place it into the candleholder and put it to one side. Pick up the picture of the animal you wish to invoke as your confidence companion. Look at the picture until you can see every line and feel the attitude of the animal.

When you feel that you know the animal well, place the picture under the candleholder and light the candle. By its light, use your black marker pen to draw your animal on the stone, using only a few lines. Pass the stone over the candle flame—feel your totem animal protecting you and feel its power fusing with the stone. Keep the stone with you whenever you feel the need for confidence.

COPING WITH LOSS AND HATRED

COPING WITH LOSS

When you are dealing with the loss of a loved one through death or the ending of a relationship, you are in effect experiencing a rite of passage. You may feel the sadness of the loss or you may be battling an almost overwhelming sense of anger, grief, or injustice. This spell focuses on the correspondence between sadness and the elements. Sadness resonates with the element of Water, and is symbolized by tears. Anger, grief, or a sense of injustice resonates with the element of Fire.

What do I need?
- A white candle
- Matches
- A stable candleholder
- Some of a favorite liqueur or a drink you shared with your loved one in the past
- A wineglass, chalice, or goblet
- A single tear

When should I do this spell?
Whenever you feel sad, but preferably on a night when the moon is waning

What should I do?
Collect your spell ingredients and set up in a place where you feel comfortable and will not be disturbed. Light the candle and put it in the candleholder, then pour the liqueur or drink into the glass or goblet.

Focus on the candle and allow yourself to feel the sadness rising within you. Save one teardrop and mix it with your drink. Take two sips only, giving one blessing to your loved one and another to the feelings you are experiencing. When you are ready, take your glass outside or stand near a window in full view of the moon.

Raise the glass above your head and feel the energy of the moon captured in the liqueur. Imagine the energy of the moon moving down your arms, through your body, and into your feet. Visualize this energy connecting with the flow of the Earth's energy. Drink the enchanted liqueur, leaving a small mouthful. Pour the remaining liqueur into the ground, imagining your sadness flowing away from you into the ground with it.

COPING WITH HATRED

This spell is designed to help you seal your home against intense
negative energies. It uses the strong psychic cleansing properties of
sea salt and the protective qualities of fennel.

What do I need?

- A cup of sea salt
- A bowl of water
- A bunch of fennel
- Black silk ribbons
- The symbol of the pentacle (optional)

When should I do this spell?

During the phase of the full moon

What should I do?

Pour the salt into the bowl of water and divide the bunch of fennel
into small bundles—as many bundles as there are windows and
external doors in your home. Tie each bundle with a black silk
ribbon.

Take the bowl of salted water and lightly sprinkle the water
around the edges of all your windows and external doors. Then
hang a bunch of fennel over each opening (window or external
door) to your house. This will help protect you and your home
from hatred and other intense emotional imbalances.

Wear the symbol of the pentacle or another talisman that has
protective qualities for you.

SPELL CRAFT TIP

Ancient wisdom

"Instead of averting your eyes from the painful events of life, look
at them squarely and contemplate them often. By facing the
realities of death, infirmity, loss, and disappointment, you free
yourself of illusions and false hopes and you avoid miserable,
envious thoughts."

—EPICTETUS, A.D. *The Art of Living*, 55–135

CRYSTALS AND SPELLS

To use the magic of precious and semiprecious stones, gather—over a period of time—the stones that speak to you about certain issues in your life or that can be used in particular spells, such as rose quartz crystal for love spells.

There are many ways of choosing your crystals or stones for spell craft. Many stones have associations with certain spells. Either use a table to work out what stone you need (see pages 20–21 as a starting point) or choose a stone that feels right in your hand when you are thinking about the spell you need to cast.

For some people, the first stone they put their hands on while focusing on the desired outcome of the spell will be the stone that represents that desire for them. Others will need to handle a number of stones before they feel certain that the stone they are holding is the right one.

With this latter technique, there is the chance of finding several stones that represent shades of a particular issue, such as financial gain through a new job or through an unforeseen circumstance.

As you collect your stones, cleanse them with salt water or in a stream to remove any negative vibrations, then store them in a special box or basket, preferably lined with material, to keep them safe. Include in your box a list of your stones and the correlation you have made between the stones and the various areas or issues in your life, or particular spells.

The stones can also be used in conjunction with the elements of Air, Fire, Water, or Earth. If you need to clear your mind about a certain issue represented by the stone, use the element of Air by placing the stone outside on a windy day—this will activate a simple spell to help you clarify what you need to do to achieve your particular desire about that issue.

If you want to strengthen your will about a particular issue symbolized by the stone, pass the stone over the flame of a candle—representing the element of Fire—and imagine the success of your wish as you stare into the flame.

If you need to release some unhappy emotions that are blocking you, invoke the power of Water by washing a stone that represents those emotions in a stream or water straight out of a tap, and visualizing the emotions similarly being washed out of your body.

If you need to stabilize the energy that the stone represents, invoke the element of Earth by burying the stone in the ground; the element of Earth will help nurture the energy so that it grows steadily and powerfully.

If you need to change your lifestyle in relation to your stone's issue, try combining your stone with the appropriate herb. Particular herbs can be used to naturally charge some stones—for example, topaz and chalcedony are magically charged by peppermint.

STONE MAGIC FOR HEALING

Semiprecious stones and gems can also be used for healing purposes. It has been suggested that the color of the stone corresponds with a particular part of the body.

Stones that are the colors of the rainbow are linked to the seven chakras or energy centers of the human body. Any stone tending toward red, such as red jasper, will strengthen and stimulate your health; blue stones, such as lapis lazuli, tend to have a calming effect.

Green stones, such as moss agate or bloodstone, are thought to be general healers—they should be used when you are in doubt about your health or as a general tonic. Use the following table as a starting point in finding the right stone to use in a healing spell.

STONE	MAGICAL PROPERTIES	HEALING PROPERTIES
agate	improves energy	strengthens vision
amethyst	aids with meditation, dream magic	strengthens nerves
bloodstone	relieves depression	reduces hemorrhages
diamond	strengthens incantations	strengthens lymph system, reduces insomnia
emerald	increases prophesying ability	improves general health
garnet	heightens sexuality	reduces anemia
jade	allows you to discover beauty	improves kidney and stomach health
lapis lazuli	increases spiritual strength	alleviates rheumatism
opal	allows you to access the spirit world	improves heart health
pearl	releases anger	strengthens nerves
turquoise	acts as a good luck charm	improves vision

DREAM SPELLS

SEE ALSO **ANTI-NIGHTMARE SPELL** ON PAGE 32
AND **AROMATHERAPY SLUMBER BLEND** ON PAGE 35.

PROTECTION OF YOUR DREAM SPACE SPELL

In this spell you will create a scented dream pillow that will protect you against evil dreams. Sleep with this amulet under your pillow during times of stress and you will find that you feel more deeply refreshed when you wake.

What do I need?

- Silk, crushed velvet or any other luxurious fabric
- The following dried herbs:
  sage
  a bay leaf
  agrimony
  mugwort
  anise
  the petals of a ranunculus (buttercup)
- A piece of amber
- A needle and thread
- A sprig of fresh rosemary
- A four-leaf clover (optional)

When should I do this spell?

During the phase of the full moon

What should I do?

Clear everything from under your bed and sweep the area. In feng shui, having clutter under your bed is thought to mean that you are sleeping on top of discarded and stagnant energy, and this will contribute to bad sleep and unhappy dreams.

Next, take all your bed linen and pillows and air them for an hour under the heat of the noonday sun. If you are doing this spell on an overcast day or during the winter, allow the light of the full moon to fall on the bed linen.

With your fabric, construct a bag large enough to contain the dried herbs and the amber bead. Fill the bag with these things then close it permanently by sewing the last seam shut. Place the bag underneath your pillow or hang it over your head from the bed head.

Place the sprig of fresh rosemary under your bed, directly below the head of the bed.

If you have a dream journal, place a four-leaf clover, if you find one, between the front cover and the first page.

The spell is done—your dreams will be safe.

A SPELL TO HALT NIGHTMARES

To wake in a state of high anxiety after a nightmare can be terribly upsetting. The effects of continual nightmares can be long lasting, and may eventually lead to sleep disturbances. Here is a magical solution that may prove effective in halting your nightmares.

What do I need?

- A sheet of purple cardboard or paper, cut diagonally to create two triangles
- A black marker pen
- Adhesive tape
- A silver-colored bowl filled with water
- A pinch of salt
- A few drops or spray of perfume
- A clove of garlic
- A raw potato

When should I do this spell?

During the phase of the waning moon

SPELL CRAFT TIP

Use jasper to ward off nightmares

If your child is afraid of the night, place a night light on their left-hand side to attract psychic protection for them. Place a piece of jasper under the light—jasper is reputed to help protect a person against evil, especially against nighttime spirits.

```
A  B  R  A  C  A  D  A  B  R  A
A  B  R  A  C  A  D  A  B  R
A  B  R  A  C  A  D  A  B
A  B  R  A  C  A  D  A
A  B  R  A  C  A  D
A  B  R  A  C  A
A  B  R  A  C
A  B  R  A
A  B  R
A  B
A
```

What should I do?

Copy the magical letters shown above onto one of the triangular
pieces of cardboard or paper. Stick the design above your bed, with
the final "A" closest to your head. Add the salt and perfume to the
bowl of water and spray or sprinkle the room at least once a week
with this mixture. Each time you sprinkle the room, recite the
following:

> Guidance and love of the universe,
>   please protect me
> From the night terrors that
>   assault me.

Rub any mirrors in your bedroom with
a little garlic and place a raw potato on a
dish underneath your bed. Replace the
potato each week, and bury the old one in the
earth, so that the negativity it has absorbed will be nullified.

DEALING WITH DIFFICULT PEOPLE SPELLS

PROTECTION AGAINST DIFFICULT PEOPLE SPELL

Projecting a sense of generosity or goodwill is a very effective way of dealing with difficult people. It is one of the cleanest ways of handling people who seem petty or who are acting in a self-centered manner.

If you are finding someone difficult to communicate with because they are angry or frustrated, carry a piece of green obsidian with you to help protect you against their negative emotions.

When talking with a difficult person, imagine a green sphere, the color of the green obsidian, shining between you. Imagine that all the words you are saying to each other are being heard through the green sphere and the sphere is filtering the harshness out of the words, making it easier for you to talk to each other.

Even as a joke, never be tempted to stick pins or other sharp objects into the image of a person—a photograph or a puppet or wax doll—as a way of stopping or "binding" them from doing any harm to you or those you love.

Binding spells link you into the destructive energy of the other person, creating a downward spiral of negative energy that will draw you in when your guard is down. Never tamper with the free will of another person unless you are prepared to pay a heavy price.

The following very simple spell will give you a sense of protection from a troublesome person. Sprinkle a circle of salt around a photograph of yourself, making sure that the circle has no gaps in it. Leave this set up for as long as you feel the need to keep apart from the troublesome person. If you wish to improve relations with the person, set up a photograph of him or her and surround the picture with a circle of flowers (those without thorns) and sweets. This will encourage a happier energy for the person.

PROTECTION AGAINST A DIFFICULT TEACHER SPELL

In this spell you are going to use the powerful forces of the planets to help you cope with difficult teachers. Often problems occur when the teacher and student fail to communicate with each other.

The following spell uses the power of the planet Mercury to help your learning and attract communication opportunities that will help resolve the issues between you and your teacher.

What do I need?

• A circular piece of white or light violet cardboard (2 in. in diameter)

• A black marker pen

• Your folder or exercise book for the class of your troublesome teacher

• Cheerful wrapping paper (preferably featuring pictures of candy)

When should I do this spell?

On a Wednesday evening

What should I do?

On your circular piece of cardboard, draw the following symbol:

This is the symbol for Mercury, which corresponds to learning, quick-wittedness, and communication skills. By drawing this sign you are inviting these qualities into your life.

To anchor these qualities to a particular subject and teacher, take your exercise book or folder and paste this talisman to the middle

of the front cover. Use cheerful wrapping paper—with realistic images of cookies, candy, and cakes, for instance—to cover the talisman and the book or folder.

This book or folder will now attract sweetness in your communication with your

teacher. Another option is to save your candy wrappers and paste them onto a piece of cardboard the same size as the exercise book, which you have already pasted your talisman to.

Cover this with plastic and place it in the middle of the exercise book or in the inside pocket of your folder. You can take it out whenever you are handing in your work for the teacher to mark. Even at this late stage, the talisman on the cover will enhance the communication of your ideas and thoughts to your teacher.

PROTECTION AGAINST A DIFFICULT BOSS

A clash of personalities or overbearing behavior from your boss can
make your working life a misery. The following spell focuses on
tying knots to cast an ancient traditional spell of protection. Each
knot will protect the psychic energy centers—the chakras—that
run through your body.

What do I need?

- A length of white cord about 35 in. long
- A square box that is big enough to hold the cord and will fit into
  your pocket or bag

When should I do this spell?

During the phase of the full moon

What should I do?

There are seven chakras running through your body. When you
have tied a knot in the white cord of protection for each psychic
energy center, you will have an effective protection against a
difficult boss.

Take the white cord and tie a knot near one end. This knot
represents your base chakra, which protects you from negative
energies undermining your support at work. The
next knot protects the second chakra, which
helps you understand others, including your
difficult boss. The following knot protects the
third chakra and shields you from the negative
impressions of others.

The fourth knot protects your heart chakra
and helps you get along with people while
stopping you from feeling hurt. The fifth knot
protects your throat chakra and enhances your
power to communicate. The sixth knot
protects your intuition from being
undermined, and the seventh knot helps you
connect with a higher power.

When you have finished knotting, place the cord
in the square box—a square box is used here because
its four corners represent the four elements: Air, Fire,
Water, and Earth. Keep the box in your pocket during
work hours or place it on your desk immediately by
your right hand.

PROTECTION AGAINST DIFFICULT COLLEAGUES

The following amulet is inspired by a feng shui cure used to shield a person from backstabbing colleagues. A cure in feng shui, the Chinese art of design and placement, helps positive energy flow into an area where energy has stagnated or where energy moves so fast that it creates a dangerous stab or poison arrow that can cause illness and disharmony.

What do I need?

• Red cardboard
• Six feng shui coins (coins that have holes in the middle)
• Glue
• A hole punch
• A red tassel

When should I do this spell?

During the phase of the full moon

What should I do?

To make this six-coin amulet, first cut out a strip of red cardboard. The strip can be up to 2 in. wide, and 6⅜–8¼ in. long, depending on the size of your coins. It is important that your strip of

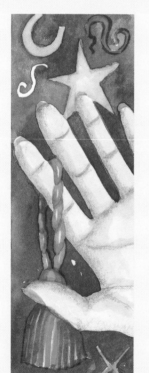

cardboard is within these size boundaries—feng shui practitioners regard these dimensions as auspicious.

Glue the coins onto the strip of cardboard, making sure you leave a little room at the bottom, then punch a hole at the bottom and tie the red tassel to the cardboard. Red is the symbol for good fortune in feng shui; in Western magic it is considered a protective and strong magical force.

Place the amulet on paperwork concerning your current work project or on the back of your chair; putting it on the back of your chair is best if your back is toward the entrance to your workspace.

EMPOWERING SPELLS

PERSONAL EMPOWERMENT SPELL: MAKING A SPELL BOX FOR YOURSELF

Making a spell box for yourself will focus your mind on what you are—it is your magical identity kit. Knowing who you really are is very powerful magic, and is an excellent protection against people who are critical or unappreciative of you.

What do I need?

- Pieces of your favorite paper and pictures
- A box, preferably made of metal, wood, or paper. It should be about 6 in. wide, between 4 in. and 6 in. deep, and up to 6 in. high—the lid of the box can be hinged or loose
- A small snippet of your hair
- A symbol of an eye with the pupil colored the color of your eyes
- Some actual nail clippings (if you like wearing a particular color nail polish, cut out the shape of your nail from a piece of balsa wood, then paint it white, then layer it with your favorite nail enamel)
- Your favorite perfume or aromatherapy oil sprinkled on some natural fabric
- Your favorite type of stone

- An example of your favorite things to do (such as a piece of your embroidery, a string from your guitar, or a drill bit)
- A picture of your favorite food
- A list, written on parchment paper, of when you like to eat, how long you like to sleep, and what you like doing

When should I do this spell?

During the phase of the full moon

What should I do?

Decorate your box with your favorite paper and pictures and then add all the other ingredients and anything else you feel will identify who you truly are. As you gather your ingredients, keep thinking of yourself as a strong, balanced person who can create whatever you truly need in your life. The spell is done.

A SIMPLE RITE TO BLESS AND EMPOWER YOUR FOOD

Perform this rite as you prepare your main meal of the day. It will release the beneficial energy of the food and allow your body to readily absorb the nourishment of this energy.

What do I need?

- A medium-sized white ceramic bowl
- A pinch of sea salt
- Four drops of rosemary essential oil
- A cup of water
- A wooden spoon about 6 in. long
- A black pen

When should I do this spell?

During your preparations for your main meal

What should I do?

Pour a generous pinch of salt into the white bowl. Salt is an ingredient traditionally used for purification and protection. In this spell, salt will act as a purifier of past unhappiness about food and your body's possible inability to absorb the nutrition from the food.

Measure out the essential oil onto the small mound of salt in the middle of the bowl. The scent of rosemary is symbolic of the element of Air, while the salt is representative of the element of Earth. Pour in the water and swirl the three ingredients together with the index finger of your left hand.

On the wooden spoon, write the initials of all the people who are going to partake of the meal you are preparing. Press hard when writing so that the pen tip cuts into the wood. Dip the wood into the water and say the following words:

I thank the world for its bounty and its nurture.
Allow the beneficial energy of the food that I am about to
prepare nourish and sustain those who partake of it.

Turn on the stove, oven, or other cooking apparatus that generates heat, and use the wooden spoon to sprinkle the water around them. Your stove represents the element of Fire, and by sprinkling the blessed Water around it you are combining the four elements to produce a balanced energy, which will flow into any food you prepare.

ENDANGERED AREA SPELL

There are many areas in the world that are suffering from neglect, poor management, and outright commercial exploitation. Try the following spell to help right the balance so that the area you are trying to help will survive. This is a major spell, and is best done with a number of people.

What do we need?

• Wooden staffs (pieces of wood that measure up to a person's shoulder) for everyone who is doing the spell
• Each person will need to collect:
  a drill
  two lengths of tan leather thong, each measuring about 15 in.
  green glass beads

earthenware (ceramic) beads

a black and white feather

a silver jump ring (a silver link from a
bead shop or a link from an old
silver necklace)

matches

a red candle

a scrap piece of cardboard

a red bag

a needle

- A picture of the endangered area
- A metal peg to anchor the picture to the ground
- A heavy stone
- A thick candle
- Matches
- A cauldron of water
- A tall "garden" incense stick or four regular-sized incense sticks

When should we do this spell?

During the phase of the full moon

What should we do?

First, each person needs to find or buy a piece of wood that
measures up to their shoulder. Drill a hole near the top, thread one
leather thong through the hole so that half the thong is on one side
of the hole and half on the other. Do the same with the second
leather thong. Each person should now have four strands on which
to thread objects that represent the four elements—Air, Fire, Water,
and Earth.

Thread the glass beads on one thread and knot the end. Use as
many beads as you like. Do the same with the ceramic beads on
another thread. Drill a hole in the quill of the feather and thread
the jump ring through it. Tie this to the end of another piece of
leather thong.

Next, light the candle. Drip the wax from the
burning candle onto the cardboard. Before the
wax sets, draw the symbol shown left on it.

When the wax disc has cooled, place it in
the red bag and tie the bag to the last strand of
leather thong.

Now all the people casting the spell must gather in a clearing
where they will not be disturbed. Mark the perimeter of a circle in

the ground and stake the picture of the endangered area onto the ground in the middle of the circle. Now quarter the circle and place, at opposite ends, the stone and the candle. On the remaining quarters, place the water and the incense stick.

Choose one person to invite the elements into the circle. He or she should first light the incense stick and say:

Powers of Air, come and join us in protecting [name of area].

Then the person should stand by the candle, light it and say:

Powers of Fire, come and join us in protecting [name of area].

Then the person should stand by the cauldron, hold their hands in the shape of a cup and say:

Powers of Water, come and join us in
protecting the world.

Then the person should stand by the stone, hold their hands out with the palms facing upward and say:

Powers of Earth, come and join us in
protecting the world.

Now you should all stand back-to-back around the picture, like sentinels, with your staffs. Visualize a blue light protecting the circle.

When you all feel ready, move to the boundary of the circle and walk around the circle, chanting the following words and stamping your staffs into the ground:

Mother of Nature, the true Holy Grail;
Father of life and of death and rebirth;
Forgive human folly, survive and prevail;
Protect lands imperiled, defend the fair Earth.

—LIAM CYFRIN

When you all feel the energy peaking, and are sure you have poured as much energy as possible into the endangered area, visualize the blue energy line dissipating. You are now free to go. Take your staffs with you, and nominate one person to keep the picture. Do this spell during each cycle of the moon until the area is saved.

EXAM PREPARATION AND PASSING SPELLS

PREPARING FOR AN EXAM

When you are studying for an exam, there is sometimes a tiny voice in your head that comes up with all sorts of criticisms about what you are doing and how you are doing it, generally undermining your preparation. If this is happening to you, try the following spell to help clear your head.

What do I need?

- A sheet of plain white paper
- A black pen
- A white envelope
- A pinch of sage
- A pinch of sea salt
- A silver bowl half-filled with sand (optional)
- Matches

When should I do this spell?

Whenever you are preparing for an exam

What should I do?

Collect your ingredients and sit quietly at your desk. Allow your mind to replay all the negative messages that you seem to be hearing. Write them down on the paper as quickly as possible so that you don't miss any. Keep writing until you are about to repeat yourself. Use more than the one sheet of paper if you need to.

Look at your list and draw a curved line right around all the words, enclosing the words within a circle. Make sure that this circle is completely closed. Fold the paper and put it into the white envelope. Put in the sage and sea salt, then seal the envelope.

Take the envelope to a fireplace or the silver bowl half-filled with sand. Light the envelope and watch it burn. See the smoke rise and imagine that the words on the page mean absolutely nothing and are as insubstantial as the smoke. The spell is done.

KEEPING PANIC AT BAY

It is important to have a good night's rest before any exam. Try to finish studying by 10:00 P.M., as this is the cutoff point for the mind taking in new information. During sleep, your mind, if it is not raddled by fear, processes the information you have fed it.

Take a few moments to do the following spell to help you go to bed in a calm frame of mind; this will help you in the exam room the next day.

What do I need?

- A purple candle
- A few drops of lavender oil
- Matches
- A stable candleholder
- A small piece of hematite
- A sprig of fresh rosemary

When should I do this spell?

The night before an exam

What should I do?

Rub the oil onto the candle and feel a sense of calm descend on you as you breathe in the scent of the lavender and feel the smoothness of the candle.

Light the candle and place it in the candleholder. Sit in a comfortable chair so that you can see the flame. Hold the hematite in your hand as you concentrate on your breathing.

Breathe in for a count of four and out for a count of four. Feel all your tensions falling away from you as you sink deeper into your chair. Hematite is an excellent stone for helping you feel grounded and free from panic.

When you feel ready, place the hematite under your pillow and the rosemary on the floor under your bed, making sure it is directly under your head. Put your main textbook for the topic of the examination in the same place.

When you wake in the morning, take the piece of hematite with you to the exam and hold it whenever you feel panicky or that you are spacing out.

FAITHFUL RELATIONSHIP SPELLS

This spell involves making a small weaving to celebrate all the
things that you bring to your relationship and to remind your
partner of all the aspects of the relationship that should not be lost.

What do I need?

- Two sticks, each about 8 in. long
- A skein of yarn in each of the seven colors of the rainbow (red,
  orange, yellow, green, blue, indigo, and violet)
- A small piece of orrisroot

When should I do this spell?

During the phase of the full moon

What should I do?

Make an equal-armed cross out of the two sticks and use some of
the red yarn to secure the sticks in the middle by tying a knot and
looping the yarn in the shape of a figure 8 around the four arms.
When the arms feel secure, use the yarn to tie the piece of orrisroot
to the center of the cross. Orrisroot is used to inspire love and long-
term relationships.

Loop the red yarn over one arm of the cross and
continue looping the yarn over and then under each arm
in a clockwise direction. Continue until you have
created a square band of red yarn about ¾ in. wide
from the center. As you are working with the red
yarn, visualize the physical security you feel with
your partner. Continue making your relationship rainbow by
tying a knot to join the colors and making new bands of color:

- Orange yarn while visualizing the creative support and sexual
  happiness you have shared together;
- Yellow yarn while visualizing the respect you have for your
  partner;
- Green yarn while visualizing the love you have for your partner;
- Blue yarn while visualizing the clear communications you have or
  wish to have with your partner;

- Indigo yarn while visualizing the respect you have for your partner's intuition; and
- Violet yarn while visualizing your partner's deeper connection with you.

Hang the weaving anywhere on the left side of the space that you share with your partner.

A SPELL TO KEEP A LOVER OR SPOUSE FAITHFUL

The following spell is a typical prescription given to a young man or woman unhappy in love in the South. The spell, roughly 100 years old, has been handed down by word of mouth, and is typical of spells from that region that are designed to keep a lover or spouse faithful.

What do I need?
- A few of your lover's hairs from a recently used hairbrush
- A decorative jar with a lid
- Enough rose water to almost fill the jar
- Seventeen teaspoons of sugar
- A teaspoon of ground ginger
- A teaspoon of ground cinnamon
- A teaspoon of ground cardamom
- A sweet-smelling essential oil, such as rose or ylang ylang
- A yellow ribbon

When should I do this spell?
During the phase of the full moon

What should I do?
Place the hairs in the jar and pour in the rose water. Add the sugar, ginger, cinnamon, and cardamom. Each ingredient has an obvious symbolic function: the rose water and sugar are intended to keep the straying lover sweet on the one casting the spell, while the ginger powder is believed to rekindle passion in the relationship. The cinnamon and cardamom powders are traditionally used in love magic to inspire thoughts of faithfulness and love.

Place the lid on the jar and then rub it with your chosen sweet-smelling essential oil. Finally, tie the yellow ribbon around the jar as a forget-me-not symbol, attracting your lover with thoughts of love. Place the jar under the bed you share with your lover.

FAMILY PROTECTION SPELLS

PROTECTING YOUR FAMILY AT HOME

The power of the name is sometimes overlooked in modern society—in ancient cultures, to know the name of a person was to have power over them. The following spell does not seek to control a member of your family through magic; it seeks only to anchor a spell for their benefit.

What do I need?

- Two pieces of parchment paper
- Two small plastic bags
- A black pen
- Two iron horseshoes
- Two heavy stones

When should I do this spell?

During the phase of the full moon

What should I do?

Ask permission from all your family living in your house to be included in this spell. If they say yes, write down their names on both pieces of the parchment paper.

Fold each piece of paper and place it in a plastic bag. Bury each bag with a horseshoe on top: one near the front doorstep and the other near the back step. If you live in an apartment, you could bury one list of names in the soil of a potted plant near the front door and one near a back window or balcony. When you have covered the spot where they are buried, place a stone on each spot.

This spell means that every time a person enters your house, through the front or back door—or stands near the back window or balcony if you live in a apartment and have used those places to bury your list of names—they are releasing a blessing for each person in the house.

PROTECTING YOUR FAMILY
WHEN THEY ARE AWAY FROM HOME

This spell is an excellent one to cast when you have a family member away from home. Although your family member is not physically present, you can still send that person a flow of protective energy.

What do I need?
• A picture of your loved one
• An attractive gilded frame
• One white candle
• One black candle
• A small crystal vase suitable for one flower stem
• Your loved one's favorite flower
• Matches

When should I do this spell?
During the phase of the full moon

What should I do?
Place the picture in the frame. The sheen of the gold will attract good luck to the person. Place the framed picture on a ledge at about eye level—a mantelpiece or a high shelf of a bookcase, for example. Place the white candle on the right-hand side of the picture (as you look at it) and the black candle on the left-hand side. The white candle, when lit, represents the attraction of positive energy to your loved one; the black candle, when lit, protects the person from negative energy. Do not get the positions of these two candles reversed.

Fill the crystal vase with fresh, clear water and place the flower in the water. For short stays away from home, change the flower every day until your loved one comes home. Light the candles at the same hour each day, and leave them to burn for one hour. If your loved one is away for a long period of time, such as two months to a year, place a potted plant, either a cyclamen or basil, near their picture.

FEELING GOOD ABOUT YOURSELF SPELL

When you feel down, try the following candle spell to reaffirm your true strength and beauty. Also, try the spell on page 167 to appreciate and tap into your true beauty! If you feel vulnerable, try some of the protection spells on pages 150–153.

What do I need?

- A really nice piece of paper
- Your favorite pen
- An essential oil or perfume of your choice
- A yellow candle
- A stable candleholder
- Matches

When should I do this spell?

During the phase of the full moon or anytime you feel down and unhappy

What should I do?

On your piece of paper, write down all the things you like about yourself. This might seem hard at first, but imagine that you have an "inner friend" who really likes you and is pointing out your good qualities or is defending you if your conscious mind comes up with some negative thoughts. List all the positive qualities you know you have. For example:

I am a careful thinker

I am a loyal friend

(or even) *I have cute toes or a nice smile!*

Rub some of your favorite essential oil or perfume over the yellow candle while reading out loud, with confidence, all the things you have written down. Place the candle in the candleholder and fold the piece of paper so that it will fit under the candleholder.

Light the candle and allow it to burn to the end; it will empower the positive thoughts about you that you wrote down. Keep the piece of paper in a safe place and take it out whenever you feel down again to remind you of your inner strength and power.

FEELING STRONG SPELL

SEE ALSO **CONFIDENCE SPELL** ON PAGE 57
AND **FIRST DAY AT SCHOOL SPELL** ON PAGE 84.

To feel confident and strong during what you think might be a difficult day, such as the day of a job interview or your first day at school, college, or work, try the following spell—it will help you tap into an image of yourself where you look good and feel strong. As you think positively of yourself, you will create a strong magical vibration that will attract positive energy, in the form of either positive people or constructive incidents.

What do I need?

• A photograph that shows you at
  your best
• A mirror
• A white candle
• Matches
• Adhesive tape

When should I do this spell?
The night before any day you feel anxious about

What should I do?
Sit or stand in front of a mirror.

Place the photograph of yourself next to, or in one corner of, your mirror. Light the white candle and place it so that you can see the candle flame in the mirror.

Breathe deeply and look at the candle flame. After a few moments, close your eyes and see the flame of the candle floating near the center of your forehead. This space is called the "Mind's Eye"—it is believed to be a gateway to your magical or intuitive self.

When you can clearly see the flame against your forehead, open your eyes and look at the photograph of yourself very carefully. What do you like about it? Look at yourself in the mirror.

Visualize the image in the photograph and the one in the mirror being one and the same. This is the image that you will project on your first day. To anchor these two images together, tape the photo to the mirror and position the mirror so that it is facing a window— the outside world. Leave the mirror in this position until you come home from your day.

FINDING SPELLS

FINDING LOST STUFF SPELL

It may be a lot easier for you to find your car keys, your Auntie Mabel's will, or your favorite ring if you do the following spell, which uses a pendulum to tap into a powerful form of wisdom—your intuition—and a bit of fairy power!

What do I need?
- A glass or metal pendant with a pointy end at the bottom hanging from a silver chain (or use a pendulum)
- A small plastic bag that the pendant or pendulum will fit into
- A small spade to dig a hole

When should I do this spell?
During the phase of the full moon

What should I do?
Place your pendant or pendulum in the plastic bag. Now go out into the garden and think—if you were a fairy, where you would like to hang out? Fairies and beneficial magical entities usually like pretty, sheltered areas where there is an attractive plant or flower.

When you have found the right place, dig a small hole (without disturbing any nearby plant) and place the pendant or pendulum, in the plastic bag, in the hole. Cover it with earth and leave it overnight. This is called "charging" an object with magical power from the Earth, the moon, and the fairies.

If you don't have a garden, fill a small terra-cotta pot with soil and bury the pendant or pendulum in that. If you can do a decent drawing, draw or paint a small picture of a fairy on the pot; if not, paste a pretty picture of one on it. Place the pot where it can catch the rays of the moon.

The next day, dig up the pendant or pendulum. It will now be able to help you find your lost treasure. Walk around the house with the pendant or pendulum swinging from your left hand. If the pendulum starts swinging quite hard by itself, you are near treasure.

FINDING THE RIGHT PLACE TO LIVE SPELL

Feng shui practitioners believe that the place we live in should have a harmonious flow of energy. It is important that the flow of energy meanders up to the front door, and that it is not obstructed within the house by awkwardly placed doors.

They believe that certain places should be avoided—houses that have been involved in a divorce settlement or in which people went bankrupt, houses near a cemeteries or churches, and houses that face an oncoming road (at a T intersection).

Even if you are not familiar with feng shui principles, you can still work out whether or not the flow of energy in a house you are inspecting is beneficial.

What do I need?

• To protect yourself from any stray negativity, carry with you an amulet of protection, such as a jade bi. A jade bi is a circular piece of jade with a hole in the middle.

When should I do this spell?

On a Saturday

What should I do?

Walk to the front door or main entrance of the premises. Hang your amulet of protection around your neck or carry it in your pocket. Take three deep breaths and try to feel the energy flowing through the front door. Let yourself be caught up in the energy flow as you wander in and out of each room in the house.

As you enter each room or area, feel or visualize the flow of energy in the room. If the energy feels slow or seems to disappear in a particular room or area, it means there is stagnant or poisoned energy there that will require clearing. Other indications of stagnant or poisonous energies include feeling a sharp chill upon first entering a room or area, decay of interior features and dead trees in the garden, or a generally claustrophobic quality to the building.

For maximum success in your life, choose a house that does not exhibit these indications of stagnant energies.

FIRST DAY AT SCHOOL SPELL

The first day at a new school or college can be a difficult day. It is the start of a completely new life and routine, with new challenges and new hopes, the chance of new friends and understanding teachers. Try the following spell to make sure that your first day will attract the optimum positive energy toward you.

What do I need?

- A piece of parchment paper
- Scissors
- A black pen
- A rubber band
- A length of red ribbon

When should I do this spell?

The night before starting at a new school or college

What should I do?

Cut up your piece of paper into 10 pieces. On each piece of paper, write down 10 things you want to happen on your first day at the new school or college, such as:

> *I want to meet a loyal friend.*
>
> *I want to find a supportive group of friends.*
>
> *I want to get understanding and respectful teachers.*
>
> *I want to get into all my preferred courses.*
>
> *I want to be seen as a friendly person.*
>
> *I want to be well thought of.*
>
> *I want to be generally well liked.*
>
> *I want to avoid feeling humiliated.*
>
> *I want to avoid being criticized.*
>
> *I want to avoid being bullied.*

Stack the 10 pieces of paper together and put the rubber band around the stack. If the paper is thin enough, roll the stack and put the rubber band around the bundle. Loop the rubber band (without breaking it, of course) so that the stack or bundle is as tightly compressed as possible. If the band breaks, start the spell all over again.

Tie the red ribbon around the stack or bundle and carry it with you the next day in your right-hand pocket.

FOCUS SPELL

If there is a question in the exam paper that has you stumped, try the following spell to help you refocus. The spell is in two stages. The first stage can be done at home, the night before the exam; the second can be done in the exam room—it won't draw attention to you.

What do I need?
- A pinch of sea salt
- Four sprigs of lavender
- Four drops of rosemary essential oil
- A small purple drawstring bag
- A small piece of lapis lazuli
- A naturally occurring pointed crystal (preferably clear quartz)
- A special black pen (a pen that you will use only for this spell)

When should I do this spell?
The night before the exam and during the exam

What should I do?
Put the salt and the sprigs of lavender into the bag. Pour the four drops of rosemary oil into the bag so that they will be absorbed by the lavender and salt. Place the lapis lazuli in the bag. Lapis lazuli corresponds to creative energy, which will help you unravel the exam question's purpose. Place the pointed quartz crystal in the bag. This stone carries a point, which means its magical intention is to help you focus on your question.

Draw the string of the bag closed. Select a pen you wish to use for the spell. Take the bag and the pen outside or to a window where you can see the moon. Show the moon your tools and say the following words:

Gentle Moon, let your light charge my tools

To help me focus on the words [numbers] I need to pass this exam.

Take the bag and pen with you to the exam. When you feel the need to focus, hold the bag, breathe in the scents of rosemary and lavender and, with your special spell pen, draw a spiral on the bag, starting from the outside and working inward. As you reach the central part of the spiral, you will feel that you have regained your focus for the exam. Good luck.

FOOD AND SPELLS

SEE ALSO **A SIMPLE RITE TO BLESS AND EMPOWER YOUR FOOD** ON PAGES 72-73.

We all know that food contains both the energy to fuel our physical bodies and the tastes to soothe our emotions. It is not often acknowledged that ordinary everyday food also has magical powers to enhance our psychic abilities.

Shamans and tribal witch doctors are no strangers to the careful use of local plants with hallucinogenic properties to enhance their abilities to access the spirit world. These plants and substances must be treated with extreme caution; they should not be needed by the disciplined practitioner of spell craft. Such potent substances are by no means necessary for magic, since what we consider everyday foods have been used for centuries for magical rituals and ceremonies designed to honor gods and goddesses. Rice, bread, sugar, and a selection of fruits and vegetables have all been used as sacraments.

If you prepare and eat food in a mindful manner, you can use the energy of the food to nurture your soul as well as your body. What is a mindful manner? It's when you take a few moments to give thanks to the energy of the Earth for providing the food you are about to eat.

The tradition of praying over a meal has its roots in the pagan past—it is carried on today in many forms of Christianity and

Judaism. Blessing food before you eat it is a way to thank the bounty of nature for supplying you with your basic needs.

In the Old World, the thanks were especially heartfelt, because our ancestors didn't always know if or when they would have another meal. Although many of us now have more certainty about this, it's still worthwhile to bless our food and invite the forces of nature into it to render it fit for both our physical and our spiritual sustenance.

Mindfulness also includes preparing and eating the food with full focus—using all your senses to appreciate the smell, taste, feel, sight, and sound of the food as it cooks. When deciding on what food to eat before a spell casting, always choose the freshest that you can afford—this will send a subliminal message to your body that you seek to treat it as a sacred space deserving of proper nurture and care. This message will color your magic work and enhance your spell craft.

Always choose food that you have found easy to digest and that leaves you feeling light and satisfied. If you are not sure of what you feel after eating certain foods, take some time out to experiment and observe your reactions to as wide a variety of food as you like.

Consider keeping a journal for a month and noting what you eat, what you feel as you are eating, and your sensations both immediately after and several hours later. Knowing yourself is a huge part of successful spell craft.

Also take into consideration the season during which you are casting your spell. Each season has its own energy, which is picked up by the fruits and vegetables that are harvested then. Also, the type of cooking enhances the energy of the season—many people find that without conscious thought, they often make stir-fries in spring, salads in summer, casseroles in autumn, and baked dishes in winter.

SPELL CRAFT TIP

The spiritual energy of food

Many of the foods we eat today are so highly processed and chemically engineered that they are almost devoid of any trace of natural energy. Such foods may nourish our bodies, but they do little for our spiritual selves. Try to eat as many organically grown and sensitively handled crops as possible—they are now becoming standard in our supermarkets.

FORTUNA OIL SPELL

Recipes for luck and success very often contain citrus-based essences, because these are said to court the favor of the mercurial energies of chance. In the following spell, the citrus flavor comes from citronella, which is often used in aromatherapy as an insect repellent. If this is not available, use essential oil of lemongrass.

What do I need?
• A glass bottle to which the following should be added:
  one part (e.g. 8 drops) frankincense absolute oil
  one part (e.g. 8 drops) lemon essential oil
  two parts (e.g. 16 drops) lavender essence
  one-eighth part (e.g. one drop) citronella essential oil
  a few whole aniseeds or saffron threads
  eight parts (e.g. 64 drops) light mineral oil as a base
• A lottery ticket
• A dripless yellow candle
• A stable candleholder
• Matches

When should I do this spell?
During the phase of the full moon

What should I do?
Combine the oils in the bottle and shake it well. Fortuna oil is especially good for anointing lucky charms, talismans, rabbit's feet, and yellow and orange candles (these are considered lucky colors). It is also said to dispose the energies of luck in your favor if you rub it on the palms of your hands before playing games of chance.

A common Puerto Rican practice is to buy a lottery ticket and place it underneath a candlestick holding a dripless yellow candle anointed with this oil. The candle should be held in the hand and

anointed from the middle of the shaft to the top and then from the middle to the base, as this symbolically invokes luck from the heavens and the manifestation of such luck on Earth. Place the candle in a prominent place, such as on a mantelpiece, and light it just before the lottery is being drawn. Good luck!

FOUR WINDS WISHING SPELL

The following spell courts the favor of the four winds, the energies of the compass points. The four winds were given magical names by the ancient Greeks—Boreas, Eureus, Notus, and Zephyrus. It is these forces, together with those of the elemental spirits of Air, Water, Fire, and Earth, that are called upon in this spell to carry your wish to the four points of the universe.

What do I need?

- Choose one of the following powdered herbs:
  bay, also known as bay laurel (for success and prestige wishes)
  rosemary (for promotion and advancement wishes)
  cinnamon (for power wishes)
  vervain/verbena (for general wishes)
  cardamom (for love wishes)
  peppermint (for prosperity wishes)
- A teaspoon
- A compass

When should I do this spell?

During the phase of the full moon

What should I do?

Measure out 4 teaspoons of your chosen herb into your left palm. Visualize your current wish as coming true. Bring your left hand near your mouth and gently breathe upon it, imagining that your wish is now traveling from your mind through your breath into the very structure of the herb.

When you are ready, go outside and turn to the north and say:

King Boreas of the North Wind, by the powers of Earth,
I call you to carry my wish to the northern quarter,
And by the powers of the gnomes,
I ask that you bring me success.

Blow a quarter of the powdered herb to the north. Do the same action for the other compass points, saying the following words:

EAST: King Eureus of the East Wind, by the powers of Air,
I call you to carry my wish to the eastern quarter
SOUTH: King Notus of the South Wind, by the powers of Fire,
I call you to carry my wish to the southern quarter
WEST: King Zephyrus of the West Wind, by the powers of Water,
I call you to carry my wish to the western quarter.

The spell is done.

FULFILL YOUR DREAMS SPELL

FOLLOWING YOUR DREAM

Often the first step to following your dream is knowing what your true dream is. A true dream is one that is yours alone—it is not part of the expectations of those around you. The following spell involves making a dream pillow. The herbs it contains will help you relax, and so allow your subconscious to find the best path toward successfully fulfilling your goals.

What do I need?

- A black marker pen with a fine point
- A bay leaf
- Gold fabric made into a bag large enough to contain the bay leaf and the herbs—you may wish to decorate the bag with a fringe
- One or more of the following dried or fresh herbs:
  anise
  agrimony
  hop
  lavender
  mugwort
  peppermint
- A needle
- Thread that matches the fabric

When should I do this spell?

During the phase of the full moon

What should I do?

Write the following words on the bay leaf with your pen:
   I follow my dream.
Place the bay leaf inside the bag and fill the bag with your herb or herbs. Neatly sew the bag shut.

   Keep the bag under your pillow for three nights. Keep a journal beside your bed and write down any dreams you can remember when you wake up.

   Review your journal after the three days and see if there are any useful tips in it on helping you follow your dream.

A SPELL TO MAKE YOUR DREAMS COME TRUE

What do you desire in life? One of the simplest ways of helping you make your dreams come true is to cast a spell that will refocus your mind so you believe that you deserve and can attain what you desire.

What do I need?

- A pillowcase (preferably light or sky blue in color)
- Yellow/orange and white fabric paints
- Silver and gold permanent marker pens
- An old pillow
- Scissors
- A handful of mint that was picked at noon and has been dried in the sun for three days
- A needle and white thread
- A dream journal and your favorite pen

When should I do this spell?

During the phase of the full moon

What should I do?

In the middle of one side of the pillowcase paint a bright sun. On either side of the sun, paint a white fluffy cloud. On the other side of the pillowcase, use your gold pen to draw the runic symbol (*left*) for making your dreams come true.

Carefully slit the old pillow a few inches along one seam and stuff the mint inside the pillow. Sew up the edge and slip the pillow into your decorated pillowcase.

When you go to bed, place your dream journal and pen on your bedside table. Sit up in bed, place your spell pillow on your lap and have the silver permanent marker pen in your hand.

Think of a dream that you wish would come true. With the silver pen, write your wish around the outside edge of each cloud. This is your silver lining on a cloud of unfulfilled dreams. Then write your wish nine times on each cloud and place the pillow near your head before going to sleep.

When you wake the next day, immediately record all the dreams and images you remember. Do this for three nights. You will soon find the path that will lead you to the dream you have chosen.

G

GAMBLING AND SPELLS

TRADITIONAL GAMBLING CHARMS

There are countless charms, roots, crystals, herbs, and formulas said to give the faithful user command over the whimsical fall of the dice or the spin of the wheel. However, such charms often have the annoying habit of working for a brief time and then suddenly ceasing to work right when the biggest win is anticipated. Perhaps this happens because there must always be a balance between good and bad fortune. Here are some of the most popular traditional gambling charms.

- A Hi John the Conqueror root (a Mexican species of morning glory from Xalapa) carried in a yellow charm bag and anointed with a commercial good luck oil is likely the most popular gambling charm in the modern world. These now-rare roots are sold in magic supply houses all over the world.
- Certain crystals and stones are said to attract luck—these include gold iron pyrites (fool's gold), aventurine, magnetite, and siderite (both of which are referred to as "lodestone") and citrine. The stones should be carried in the purse or wallet for luck.
- Lodestones, which are natural magnets, are very popular gambling charms and are generally carried in pairs in small yellow or gold cloth bags. They are carried in pairs because one lodestone draws good luck and the other banishes misfortune. The stones must be fed with iron filings or magnetic sand and the bags they are carried in should be anointed with a lucky formula, such as Fortuna Oil (see page 88).
- A traditional New Orleans charm consists of a nutmeg with a hole bored halfway into its surface. The hole is filled with mercury or quicksilver then

plugged with molten wax. Do not try to make this at home—
mercury (quicksilver) is highly toxic and should never come into
contact with the skin, eyes, or mouth.
- A red flannel or chamois bag containing a wishbone (from the
back of a chicken), a pebble taken from a graveyard and a ginseng
root is said to draw strong good fortune.

GOOD LUCK IN GAMES OF CHANCE SPELL

If you occasionally dabble in games of chance, you probably already
have your own little ritual to help improve your chances. You may
have a favorite ring that you always wear to bring you luck, or you
always bet on a particular number because you feel it is your lucky
number.

There are many traditions concerning how to attract Lady Luck
to you. As she is known to be fickle, you need to rely on your
instincts when it comes to how long you play a game, when you
move on to another game, and when you simply go home.

Feeling that you are becoming obsessed with the next turn of the
card is a very clear indication that you have lost access to your
instincts. Go home immediately. The best time to gamble is when
you feel detached and can sense the flow of energy around the
room or track. Try the following spell to help you keep in
touch with your instincts.

What do I need?
- A key
- A piece of carnelian
- A gold or silver silk bag

When should I do this spell?
On a Wednesday

What should I do?
Hold the key in your right hand if you are right-handed and
in your left hand if you are left-handed. It is the key that will help
you "unlock" your instincts if you get into a rut when gambling.

Visualize this key opening a door, through which you see
yourself winning a game without seeming to try or care. Touch this
key and it will help you move away from any potentially destructive
behavior. It will also help you focus properly again.

Place the key and the carnelian in the silk bag. The carnelian will
encourage the voice of your intuition to assert itself when you are
feeling a bit too mesmerized by the game.

GUARDIAN ANGEL SPELLS

CALLING YOUR GUARDIAN ANGELS SPELL

There are a great many ways a guardian angel can be called to give you guidance and inspiration. When you are embarking on a dangerous road, or starting a project that you feel you need divine inspiration for, consider calling your guardian angels to help you.

What do I need?

- A bowl of salted water
- A chalice filled with water
- A stick of frankincense incense
- Your favorite stone or a pebble you have found on a beach
- A white candle
- Matches
- A piece of jet
- A piece of clear quartz crystal

When should I do this spell?

During the phase of the full moon

What should I do?

Imagine a circle of blue light around you that is as big as the room you are in. Purify the circle by sprinkling the salted water around the inside perimeter of the circle. Quarter your circle and place the chalice of water and incense opposite each other, at the edge of the circle, and your favorite stone and the candle on the other two quarters. Walk to the incense stick and light it, saying the following words:

Powers of Air, bring to me my guardian angel.

Walk to the candle and light it, saying the following words:

Powers of Fire, bring to me my guardian angel.

Walk to the chalice of water and lift it, saying the following words:

Powers of Water, bring to me my guardian angel.

Walk to the stone and lift it saying the following words:

Powers of Earth, bring to me my guardian angel.

Sit in the middle of your circle with the jet in your left hand and the clear quartz crystal in your right hand. The jet, being black, will help you tap into your intuition and psychic power; the clear quartz crystal will receive the wisdom of your guardian angel.

Visualize a form of energy swirling around you. Keep this visualization going until you feel the presence of your guardian angel. Because you are doing this spell within a circle that has been purified, you will not attract any malevolent energy forms. When you feel ready, ask for your guardian angel's advice or help. Feel the vibrations of its support and nurture in the crystal in your right hand. This anchors the loving support of your guardian angel into the crystal, which you can carry with you whenever you need it.

To close the circle, walk to each quarter and thank each element for bringing you your guardian angel. Visualize the blue of the circle fading. You now have a powerful ally in your life.

CALLING A CHILD'S GUARDIAN ANGEL SPELL

The following spell is designed to invite a beloved child's guardian angel to provide a shield of protection through which the taunts and cruelty of a bully cannot penetrate.

What do I need?

- A white candle
- Matches
- A glass of water
- A white feather
- A white moonstone or piece of milky quartz

When should I do this spell?

On a Sunday evening

What should I do?

With the child's help, arrange the items neatly on a table or bench. Light the candle and close your eyes. Recite the following:

Great and pure loving spirit of guidance and protection
Angel assigned to this my child [child's name] please be here as a
Beacon of strength and mighty vigilance
Let no threat or malice harm [child's name],
And shield him/her with your wings.

Place the moonstone or white crystal in the water and dip the feather into the water. Using the feather, sprinkle some of the water over the child's head and say the following:

With this sacred water of love and power I protect you
In the name of your guardian angel who looks over you
And protects you with mighty wings.

Blow out the candle and have the child carry the crystal or moonstone at all times. Remember to thank the guardian angel when the threat has passed.

GETTING WHAT YOU WANT SPELLS

GETTING ACCEPTED SPELL

Getting yourself accepted as a participant in a particular project requires eloquence and persuasiveness. To enhance these skills, you may wish to invoke the help of the energy that resonates with the planet Mercury. The following spell gives instructions on how to make a Mercury talisman.

What do I need?

- A sturdy piece of cardboard about 5 in. square
- Your favorite pen
- A purple bag big enough to contain the ingredients of the spell
- Eight unshelled hazelnuts
- Eight coffee beans in a small plastic bag
- A small piece of amethyst

When should I do this spell?

On a Wednesday

What should I do?

On the cardboard, draw a square that contains 64 smaller squares (each side will have 8 squares) and write the following numbers in the correct positions:

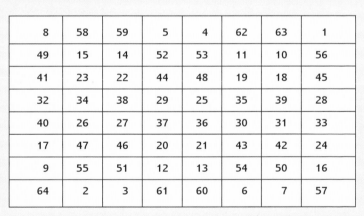

8	58	59	5	4	62	63	1
49	15	14	52	53	11	10	56
41	23	22	44	48	19	18	45
32	34	38	29	25	35	39	28
40	26	27	37	36	30	31	33
17	47	46	20	21	43	42	24
9	55	51	12	13	54	50	16
64	2	3	61	60	6	7	57

When you have finished, place the cardboard into your bag with the hazelnuts, coffee beans, and amethyst. There must be eight coffee beans and eight hazelnuts because each row of this magic square adds up to 260 (2+6+0 = 8). If your wish involves the signing of a contract or other document—if your bid was accepted or a publisher wants to publish your book, for example—sign the document with the pen you used in this spell.

GETTING PICKED SPELL

If a special project in your workplace interests you—or could ultimately lead to further recognition or a promotion—or if you are submitting a proposal or wooing a prestigious client, cast the following spell to help you stand out from the pack.

The spell involves making a success amulet that can be worn next to your skin during business meetings and when you are working on your proposal.

What do I need?

- A wooden disc measuring 2 in. in diameter
- A black marker pen
- A picture of an eye
- A gold metallic marker pen

When should I do this spell?

When you first start working toward getting the job or being part of the project

What should I do?

Mark the center of the disc with a dot with your black marker pen. Draw two lines that pass through the center, one vertical and the other horizontal, making an equal-arm cross.

In the middle of the disc, over the center dot, paste the picture of an eye. The eye wards off negative vibrations which may badly affect your chances of acquiring the job. Consider cutting out the image of an eye from the picture of one of your favorite successful people.

In each quadrant, write the following words:

Courage

Eloquence

Wisdom

Persistence

Around the edge of the disc, draw a circle of gold. Carry this disc with you until you are successful in obtaining the job or joining the project team.

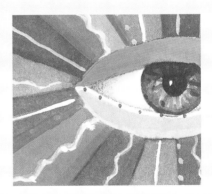

HARMONY SPELLS

HARMONY AT HOME SPELL

Squabbles, arguments, and other forms of anger in the family are all very hurtful and distracting. You should not expect that you can solve the problems of your family by yourself, but the following spell can be cast to send some positive energy into your home.

What do I need?

- A small, covered silver bowl
- Sprigs of lavender
- An item connected with each family member
- A small piece of an old dish towel
- A pinch of sea salt
- A rose quartz stone (preferably heart shaped)
- An amethyst stone (preferably circular)
- A piece of hematite (preferably circular)
- Glue

When should I do this spell?

During the phase of the full moon

What should I do?

In your silver bowl place the sprigs of lavender, one for each family member (including yourself). Lavender helps alleviate stressful and disharmonious situations.

Also place in the bowl an item connected with each family member. This can be anything small that you can lay your hands on. For example, you may take a lock of your own hair, maybe some of your mother's favorite face powder (not too much) and a drop or two of your father's aftershave.

When you have found all these items and put them in the bowl, add a snip from the dish towel. The dish towel symbolizes the meals that have been taken together as a family. Sprinkle the sea salt over the entire contents. This represents the cleansing of negative energy.

Then place the stones in the bowl, after they have been washed under running water and dried with a clean cloth. Rose quartz resonates with friendly energies, amethyst corresponds to happiness, and hematite has a healing quality and is known for its protection from negativity.

When this is done, dab spots of glue around the edge of the bowl and glue the cover onto the bowl. Place the bowl as close as possible to the front door. If you have a hall mirror, see if you can position the bowl so that it is reflected in the mirror. This will double the power of the spell.

HARMONY IN THE NEIGHBORHOOD SPELL

Arguments and disputes with your neighbors can cause great irritation. Falling fence lines, branches falling over boundary lines, and other incursions into your land can cause long-standing disharmony. However, these disputes need to be resolved, because the negative energy directed across your boundaries may weaken the natural protection of both your houses.

What do I need?
- A water feature
- A pump
- A stone or colored ball
- Goldfish (optional)
- Water plants (optional)
- A black marker pen

When should I do this spell?
During the phase of the full moon

What should I do?
This spell involves making a garden water feature that faces your neighbor's property. If you live in an apartment, you could set up a water feature on the actual common wall between you and your problem neighbor.

Use a pump to keep the water constantly moving. Water is an element that resonates with emotions. If water is stagnant, the old emotions will continue.

If the water is kept moving, this allows the emotional irritation to disperse and brings new energies to help resolve disputes and disharmony.

You may wish to plant protective herbs such as basil around your water feature—just make sure that the aspect is correct for them. Lush growth will provide abundant protective energy for you.

Draw the runic symbol (*right*) on the stone or colored ball, and place it near the water feature, or tucked within the herbs or plants around it.

HEALING SPELLS

HEALTH PROTECTION SPELL

Casting spells to protect the space that is your body is as important as casting spells to protect your wealth. It's a good idea to use both traditional and alternative methods to improve your health, keep fit, and strengthen your immune system. The following spell focuses on constructing a traditional talisman to help you protect your health; it will also encourage you to think of ways of getting fit and staying healthy.

What do I need?
- A copper disc about 2 in. in diameter
- A black marker pen or an engraving tool
- Tracing paper
- Carbon paper to transfer the design

When should I do this spell?
On a sunny Sunday

What should I do?
Gather your ingredients and take them outside in the sun. Leave the disc out in the sun at the height of the sun's powers—usually around noon—and leave it there until the disc feels warm or hot to the touch.

Allow the disc to cool down. Draw the symbol, shown above, on the disc or, using tracing paper, trace the image and transfer it onto the copper disc using carbon paper. Strengthen the outline by going over the lines with your pen.

Keep the talisman with you, particularly when you visit the doctor for a checkup or if you need to do some tests at a hospital.

HEALING RIFTS AND QUARRELS

If arguments occur between two people on a regular basis, there are likely a number of deep-seated problems in their relationship. Sometimes these arguments have nothing to do with the real problem—they are like a smokescreen that hides the real issues.

The bad feeling that is created tends to accumulate over time and can, in itself, predispose you and your partner, family member, or friend to have fights. This accumulation of an atmosphere of anger and frustration must be cleared before a real healing of the relationship can begin.

What do I need?
• Smudge stick made from good-quality sage
• Two heavy sticks (or clapping sticks)
• A copper bowl half-filled with sand

When should I do this spell?
During the phase of the new moon

What should I do?
At the start of a new phase of the moon, early in the morning, light the smudge stick and carry it around the house, walking in a counterclockwise direction. You may walk around the outside of the house or follow the walls on the inside.

Place the smudge stick in the copper bowl and let it smolder in the center of the house. Now pick up your two heavy sticks.

Go to each of the places where arguments occur. Walk to the nearest corner to each spot and loudly hit your sticks together. Imagine that you are scaring the arguments out of the house and giving the people in the house a chance to communicate properly.

When you have used the sticks in all the relevant corners, take your smudge stick and make sweeping motions, visualizing that you are moving and cleansing the bad energy out of the house and out of your lives.

HERBS AND SPELLS

SEE ALSO **CELESTIAL BODIES AND SPELLS** ON PAGES 46–47.

Herbs have been used in spell craft since ancient times. Over this long period of time, many herbs were found to have beneficial effects on healing spells as well as on other spells, ranging from spells for finding love to spells for enhancing the protection of a person or their home.

A number of prominent herbalists of the past centuries were also interested in astrology, in the influence of the celestial bodies over human beings, as well as plants. Dr. Nicholas Culpepper, a prominent herbalist of the early seventeenth century and still known for his *Complete Herbal*, was also an astrologer.

Below is a table of herbs that can be included in spells that are powered by cosmic links with a particular celestial body.

Herbs to be used for healing and for spell craft should be picked during the peak of their psychic energy, either during the most

powerful phase of the moon—the full moon— or during the height of the sun's energy, at summer solstice. Traditionally, herbs are cut at full moon if they are to be used for a healing spell. However, if the spell is to help eliminate the presence of disease or discomfort, the herbs are cut during the phase of the waning moon. Herbs for success in a new relationship or business venture are cut during a new moon.

CELESTIAL BODIES	CORRESPONDING HERBS
Sun	chamomile, cinnamon, frankincense, marigold, saffron, St. John's wort, sunflower
Moon	coriander, ginger, jasmine, lily, moonwort, white rose, rowan
Mercury	caraway, dill, fennel, flax, honeysuckle, lavender, parsley
Venus	bergamot, clover, gardenia, golden seal, pennyroyal, thyme, verbena
Mars	basil, chives, coriander, cumin, garlic, horseradish, tarragon
Jupiter	agrimony, borage, cardamom, dandelion, myrrh, sage, sandalwood
Saturn	arnica, belladonna, comfrey, hemlock, pokeroot, Solomon's seal, witch hazel

TYPE OF SPELL	HERBS USED
Protection	angelica, chamomile, cumin, dill, fennel, frankincense, garlic, ginger, hyssop, St. John's wort
Love	clover, cloves, feverfew, lemon balm, lovage, marshmallow, pennyroyal, peppermint, raspberry, tarragon
Luck and success	acorn, aloe, chamomile, cinnamon, clover, frankincense, hollyhock, mint, musk, myrrh
Prosperity	basil, cowslip, ginger, honeysuckle, marjoram, moneywort, myrrh, nutmeg, sesame, vetiver
Inner peace	agrimony, borage, camphor, chamomile, coriander, mistletoe, myrrh, parsley, sage, valerian

The table above provides a list of the most common herbs associated with some of the most common types of spells. Some herbs appear in more than one column because they have more than one magical use.

SIMPLE MAGICAL HERBAL TEA SPELLS

Making a herbal tea is a great way of using the power of an enchanted herb. Teas are made by pouring a cup of boiling water over a teaspoon of a powdered herb and allowing it to steep for three to five minutes. Strain the tea and place your hand over it. Close your eyes and say a simple prayer, asking that the tea bring the desired energy into your life. When the tea has cooled a little, drink it. Here are some traditional recipes:

Negative energies
• To ward off negative energies, try sage tea—it is highly protective.

Loving energies
• To encourage loving energies, try a mixture of orange rind, rose hip, and cinnamon. This makes a delicious love tea, especially with a little honey. Also try placing a copper coin in the teapot as the tea steeps; this is the metal of the astrological planet Venus, symbolic of love and romance.

Luck and opportunity
• To attract luck and opportunity, make lemongrass tea and place an almond in the teapot to pay homage to the astrological planet Mercury, whose domain is chance.

Wealth and abundance

• To draw wealth and abundance, try a mixture of one part ginger, and one-eighth parts each of clove and nutmeg.

Courage

• For courage, especially when you are feeling threatened, use herbs such as parsley, raspberry leaf, nettle, aniseed, and ginger.

HONORING YOURSELF SPELL

This is a nurturing spell that creates a loving energy field that wraps around you, protecting and nourishing you. It is based on a guided meditation that encourages you to feel loved and cherished. This feeling is anchored into a stone that you can carry with you in times of loneliness, trouble, or unhappiness.

What do I need?

• A comfortable chair
• An oil burner filled with water
• A tea light
• Matches
• Four drops of lavender essential oil
• Four drops of rose geranium essential oil
• A small amethyst
• A purple bag (made of natural fiber) that is large enough to contain the amethyst

When should I do this spell?

Anytime you are feeling down

What should I do?

Prepare your oil burner by measuring out the lavender and rose geranium essential oils and lighting the tea light. Sit comfortably in your chair and hold the amethyst in your hand.

Concentrate on your breathing: breathe in for a count of four and out for a count of four. When you feel ready, imagine that you are standing in a beautiful glade covered with soft grass and dappled sunlight. A dense forest surrounds the glade.

Visualize that a beloved family member or friend is walking through the trees to join you in the glade. This person can be someone who is alive or someone who has passed away. Embrace the person and let them stand near you. Now imagine that other people are coming toward you—everyone you know who cares for you is coming. Allow your conscious mind to invite those you do not know yet but who will be important to you in the future. Embrace each one and watch them all form a circle around you.

Visualize the energy emanating from this circle enfolding you in a pure light. Allow yourself to feel deeply joyful and warmly appreciated. Feel this energy concentrating into your amethyst.

When you are ready, say goodbye to your circle of loved ones and concentrate again on your breathing. Open your eyes and feel the glow of energy from your stone. Place it into its purple bag and extinguish the tea light in the oil burner. Keep the amethyst in its bag under your pillow to give you a restful night's sleep.

HOUSE PURIFICATION SPELL

When you are taking possession of a new home it is wise to cleanse the premises of energy left over from the previous tenants. The following European spell will help you clear this energy from your new house.

What do I need?
- A white candle
- A stable candleholder
- Matches
- A stick of sweet-smelling incense
- A glass bowl of salted water
- Some of the type of bread you usually eat
- A bell, preferably with a sweet ring

When should I do this spell?
Just before moving into your new home

What should I do?
Arrange the items in a circle around you in the part of the house you consider the psychic hub of the dwelling—perhaps the kitchen or the family room. While sitting comfortably in the middle of the circle, light the candle and the incense. Relax, breathing deeply for a moment to ground yourself. When you feel ready, pick up the bowl of water and say:

With this salt and water
I purify this place of all but the most pure and beneficent energies.
Walk about the entire dwelling, sprinkling the water as you go. Return to the circle and place the bowl in its position in the circle.

Pick up the candle and say:

With this light

I bring truth and wisdom to this place.

Walk about the home with the candle, then return to the circle, placing the candle in its position. Pick up the bell and say:

With this bell

I call forth love and joy to this place.

Ring the bell as you move about the home. Again, return to the circle and place the bell in its position. Next, take the bread and say:

With this bread

I call forth abundance and prosperity to this place.

Leave small chunks of bread in every room. Return to the circle and place any bread that remains in its position. Finally, pick up the incense and say:

With this sweet perfume

I bring peace and harmony to this place.

Walk about the home, wafting smoke into every corner. Return to the circle, replace the incense and relax. Feel the energies moving and circulating within the home. When you are ready, blow out the candle and put away all the items you used in the spell. Leave the chunks of bread strewn about the home overnight—remove them in the morning.

I

INNER SANCTUARY SPELLS

CREATING AN INTERNAL SANCTUARY

When things become too much and you need to get away, you can create a sanctuary in which you can find peace and safety in your own home. This type of spell creates a safe place for you—it is only limited by your imagination.

What do I need?
- Three of the following herbs as potted plants:
  caraway
  dill
  garlic
  parsley
  pepper
  rosemary
- Blue mosaic pieces or squares, enough to form a circle around the herbs
- A spot in the garden to plant these three herbs or a suitable pot and potting mix so that the plants can be indoors, near a window or on a balcony

When should I do this spell?
During the phase of the new moon

What should I do?
Plant the three chosen herbs in your garden or in your pot. If you are using a pot, choose one made from natural materials, such as terra-cotta. Do not use a plastic pot.

When you have planted the herbs, take your blue mosaic pieces or small tiles and form a circle in the soil around them. Sit near the mosaic circle in a comfortable position. If you can smell the herbs, focus on the scent. If you can't smell them, buy some ready-to-use herbs and breathe in their scent.

As you smell the herbs and focus on the circle, visualize being in your ideal garden with these plants in it. How does this garden or sanctuary look? Is there a waterfall? Is there a pond with goldfish? Is there a pine forest in the background? Is the soil rich and the grass lush? Visualize the garden in as much detail as you can, creating as beautiful a sanctuary as you can imagine.

When you are ready, imagine that the entrance to your sanctuary is through the circle of blue mosaic tiles. Tend your garden well and use this vision whenever you need to retreat to a safe place.

A CHARM FOR FINDING YOUR INNER SANCTUARY

Often life seems to become too complicated, and moves at too frantic a pace. The following spell will help you find a retreat where you can let go of your worries and refocus on your sense of inner peace and psychic balance.

What do I need?
• A comfortable towel, blanket, pillow, or cushions
• Four drops of eyebright tincture
• A handful of salt in a container (such as a mortar and pestle)
• A symbol of the sun—at the very least a gold disc made from metal or cardboard
• A symbol of the moon—at the very least a silver crescent made from metal or cardboard (or a piece of moonstone)

When should I do this spell?
Anytime you feel stressed

What should I do?
Find a place in your home or garden where you can have some quiet time to yourself and set up a space there where you can sit with comfort and ease. Measure out the eyebright tincture into the salt and grind it into the salt. Eyebright helps us see the joyous side of life and encourages us to increase our psychic visualization skills.

Sprinkle the tinctured salt around you in a circle—this creates a safe barrier between you and the world. When you are ready, hold the sun symbol in your right hand and the moon symbol in your left hand, and visualize the power of the sun and moon emanating from your hands. Visualize the energy of the sun and moon as colors, and imagine these colors merging to create a picture of your inner sanctuary. Take time to imagine what your perfect sanctuary would look like. Be at peace in this space and know that you are able to think and breathe freely here.

Enjoy this space for however long you wish; when you return to the everyday world you will feel refreshed and balanced.

INTUITION AND SPELLS

SPECIAL DEDICATION TO YOUR INTUITION

Intuition is an essential part of spell craft. We all have the ability to hear from our higher selves how to make the right decisions, but first we must learn to still our minds. When we stop our minds' continual chatter we can hear the softer tone of our inner voice— the voice of our higher self, that part of us that is connected to the rest of humanity and to the universe itself.

One of the easiest ways of quieting your mind is to use meditation techniques. For example, sit quietly in a comfortable chair by the light of a candle. Close your eyes and take three deep breaths—in through the nose and out through the mouth. Silently repeat the following:

I dedicate this moment to the powers of pure white light and allow
The stream of universal energy to course through me
Unhindered by trivial and harmful thoughts.
This quiet moment connects me to the core of creative energy.

Take ten deep breaths, counting backward from ten to one. When you are ready, open your eyes and begin your day—or use this peaceful moment to begin a spell.

If you practice this meditation technique every day, you will find that it has marvelous effects. It can open your eyes to the beauty that exists everywhere but is so often unnoticed. It can help make you feel— and even look—more youthful. Most importantly, it allows the truth of your higher self to be unveiled. Learn to trust your insights, and in time you will find that the voice of your intuition will be clear and unmistakable.

MAKING AN INTUITION POUCH

One of the most important ways of strengthening your intuition
is to believe in it and to set aside some time to sit quietly and see
or listen to your inner thoughts. Traditionally, your intuition is
stronger when the moon is either dark or full. At the next dark
moon, make an intuition pouch to help you tune into your deepest
thoughts.

What do I need?

- Choose three of the following oils:
  cloves, patchouli, sandalwood, frankincense
- Choose three of the following herbs:
  bay laurel, cinnamon, cloves, mugwort
- A small glass bowl
- A low table covered with
  a clean cloth
- A dark blue candle
- A small circular piece of dark
  blue cloth
- A length of black string or
  embroidery thread
- Matches
- A comfortable cushion to sit on

When should I do this spell?

The last day of the waning moon (the dark moon)

What should I do?

Mix the oils and herbs in the bowl and place it on the table along
with the candle, the piece of cloth and the string or embroidery
thread. Light the candle and turn out the lights. Sit in front of the
table on a cushion and look into the light. Relax, calm your mind,
and focus on the light of the candle. When you feel ready, place the
pile of the herbs onto the cloth, saying the following words:

Open the starlit veil of night,
So I may see with inner sight;
By magic's art, reveal to me,
The hidden things I wish to see.

Gather the cloth up, with the herbs still inside, and tie the ends
together, so that it makes a pouch, with the string or embroidery
thread. Wear your pouch at times when you want your intuition to
be at its strongest.

INVISIBILITY SPELLS

There are many traditional invisibility spells. However, like most traditional spells, they involve some rather gruesome and often unobtainable ingredients. Modern invisibility spells are predominantly geared toward making you virtually invisible—they will make you unnoticeable rather than truly invisible.

INVISIBILITY SPELL 1

One of the simplest invisibility spells is to imagine a blue light surrounding you when you feel the need to be invisible. The following spell empowers your sense of invisibility by invoking the elements of Earth, Air, Fire, and Water.

What do I need?

- A blue feather
- A blue stone (blue agate)
- A picture of the ocean
- A blue cloth bag with a drawstring
- A blue candle
- Matches
- A piece of cardboard
- A pin
- A piece of quartz crystal

When should I do this spell?

During the phase of the new moon

What should I do?

Facing west, place the blue feather, blue stone, and the picture of the ocean into the bag. These symbolize the elements of Air, Earth, and Water. The color blue is traditionally used in magic for obtaining peace and quiet. Light the blue candle and drip some wax onto the

---

SPELL CRAFT TIP

A magic circle

Before performing a spell, cast yourself a magic circle by visualizing a glove of electric blue flame around you and your spell-working space. This will help focus and contain the energy you raise within your spell.

---

cardboard. When the wax has almost dried, draw on it with your pin the rune shown at right:

This rune, called algiz, has a protective quality. While the wax is still slightly moist, peel it off the cardboard without breaking it. Leave it to dry and then put it into your bag.

When you combine these objects in your drawstring bag, you are invoking the power of the elements. As the combination of these elements is believed to make up this world, this spell will help you blend into the background when you do not wish to be noticed.

INVISIBILITY SPELL 2

This spell, which will help make you inconspicuous, weaves a white ribbon of protection with blue ribbons of peace and purple ribbons of power.

What do I need?

- A white ribbon and other ribbons that are your favorite shades of blue and purple
- A symbol of a silver crescent moon
- A needle and white thread
- A white bag big enough to carry the ribbons and the moon image

When should I do this spell?

During the phase of the new moon, or anytime you feel the need for invisibility

What should I do?

If you can't purchase a silver symbol of the crescent moon, make one out of cardboard and tin foil. Draw the symbol of the crescent moon on cardboard and cut it out. Cover the cutout with sheets of tin foil. Punch a hole into one end of the symbol.

Take the three ribbons and braid or twist them together. Sew your silver crescent moon symbol to the end of one of the ribbons. Tie a knot at the other end of the braid or twist so that your ribbons do not unravel. Place the ribbons and moon image in the white bag and carry the bag with you when you wish to be invisible. Remember to keep the bag at home when you want to be noticed!

INVESTING MONEY WISELY SPELL

If you wish to invest, you need time, information, and expertise to ensure that you make the right decisions and do not fall prey to "get-rich-quick" schemes. However, you also need a bit of luck. This spell is designed to help you tap into a form of universal intelligence that will help you decide when to invest and whose advice to heed.

What do I need?
• A statement from your investment account, when the account had in it the largest amount of money from an investment ever, or a blank piece of paper
• A crystal pendulum hanging from a chain

When should I do this spell?
Anytime you think of, or are told of, an investment venture

What should I do?
Take a photocopy of the bank statement or, if you bank electronically, write on a piece of paper the full amount of the largest sum of money in your account. This represents a history of success. If you do not have an investment portfolio, write on the piece of paper the amount of money you want to get as a return on your investment.

Now hold the chain from which the pendulum is hanging between your thumb and forefinger. If you are not familiar with using pendulums, play with it for a while, asking it which way is "yes" and which way is "no." The pendulum will start swinging, moving in a particular direction in response to each question. Keep a notebook with you to record its movements. Check that the movement for "yes" is the same a few minutes later.

When you are ready, place your elbow on the table so that you can comfortably hang the pendulum over the bank statement or piece of paper. Now ask a question, such as:

Shall I invest [insert amount] in this project?
Shall I follow [insert name]'s advice?

Keep a record of the pendulum's responses, and if you decide to act on the pendulum's responses, keep records of how those investments fare. You may wish to try out this method on small investments before using it to help you make more important investment choices.

IS MY LOVER RIGHT FOR ME SPELL

This spell focuses on using a pendulum. A pendulum enables you to tap into a form of universal intelligence that can answer your question of whether or not your lover is the right person for you. This is a useful spell if you are caught between conflicting pieces of advice, because it helps you make a decision based on your own instincts.

What do I need?
• A crystal pendulum hanging from a chain
• An article of clothing or a lock of hair from your lover

When should I do this spell?
On a Friday evening

What should I do?
Hold the pendulum between your thumb and forefinger. If you are right-handed, hold it in your right hand. If you are left-handed, hold it in your left hand. Place the item from your lover on the table near the elbow of the hand holding the pendulum, so that the pendulum hangs from its chain directly over it.

If you are not familiar with using a pendulum, take some time to get the feel of it. Ask it questions that require a "yes" or a "no" answer. For example, try asking it the following question:

Is my name [insert your real name]?

Observe which way the pendulum swings. This will be the direction of the "yes" swing. Do a similar exercise to identify the "no" swing.

When you are ready, focus on your breathing and let go of all your everyday concerns, focusing only on the question you are going to ask. When you feel in a deep, meditative state, ask the following question:

Is [insert name of lover] the right person for me at this time?
The pendulum will give you an answer. You may then ask it other questions concerning your relationship to give you further insight into what is or is not right for you.

LEARNING TO LISTEN SPELL

Try this spell to renew your ability to listen to a person who is close to you with love and goodwill, and without feeling negativity. The two of you should do this spell together.

What do I need?
• Two blue comfy cushions or chairs covered with blue cloth
• A small table
• Two blue or purple candles
• A stick of lavender incense
• Matches
• A plate of sweet cookies (home-baked, if possible)
• Two cups or glasses of hot chocolate, a good-quality coffee or a liqueur
• A melodious-sounding hand bell
• Two pieces of blue or purple cloth made from natural fiber

When should I do this spell?
Whenever you feel tension in a relationship or friendship, but if you want to tap into a time when psychic channels are open, do this spell during the phase of the full moon

What should I do?
Position the cushions or chairs so that they are opposite each other with the table between them. Make sure that there is enough space to walk around them and that neither has its back to a door. Place the candles, incense, plate of cookies, and drinks on the table.

Ask the other person to sit on a cushion or chair, then walk around the cushions/chairs in a circle three times, ringing the hand bell to disperse negativity. Try to leave arguments outside the circle.

Light the candles and incense, then sit down and drink and eat in silence together, becoming aware of the

energy between you. Allow the sweetness of the tastes to flavor the energy flow, changing it from a negative emotion to a deeper, more loving one.

When you are both ready, blow out the candles and extinguish the incense. Imagine the circle around you dissipating. Wrap each candle in a piece of cloth; give one to your partner or friend. Light this candle whenever you want to be listened to.

You can also do this spell on your own. If you do, you will need only one drink.

LEARNING TO TRUST SPELL

This is a fun spell that you can do with your partner. It will also help revive your relationship by attuning all your senses to each other.

What do I need?
• Each of you choose a sample of your favorite foods and drinks, music, soft-textured material, feathers, and scents
• A blindfold

When should I do this spell?
During the phase of the full moon

What should I do?
Choose a time when you will not be disturbed. Take the phone off the hook. Sit in a comfortable area—on the bed, or on cushions on the floor, perhaps—and arrange the favorite things you have collected around you.

Blindfold your partner. Play a piece of your favorite music, and while it is playing present him or her with one or more of your perfumes or favorite aromatherapy essential oils. Glide fabrics over his or her skin and feed him or her the choicest samples of your favorite foods or a sip of your favorite drink.

Take off the blindfold, look into your partner's eyes and drink in the beauty of your love for this person. Then let your partner blindfold you and show you his or her favorite things.

This lovely, bonding spell can be improved with the addition of kisses between each sensation shared.

LOVE AND SPELLS

THE POWER TO ATTRACT LOVE: TRADITIONAL SPELLS

Many types of love spells have evolved over the ages, because attracting love is one of our most fundamental needs. This imperative has launched a bewildering number of spells to help us find out who our ideal love is.

There are also many spells that will make a person fall in love with the spell caster or that will punish a person who has strayed. These types of spells must be avoided at all costs. It is important to remember that any negative energy you send out to harm or manipulate another will rebound on you three times. Do not tempt fate!

Traditional love spell ingredients often include herbs that act as stimulants, such as Solomon's seal and mandrake. Other herbs and spices often used in love potions are thought to heat the blood, which in turn is believed to arouse the passions.

The goddess Venus and the ruling planet of Venus have strong traditional associations with love and love spells. The various stones, colors, and metals that correspond to the energy of this planet are believed to empower love spells.

Here is a traditional spell that lets you see your prospective husband or wife. Sit in front of a mirror during Halloween (October 31) and gaze at the forehead of your reflection. Say the following words:

Mirror, mirror,
Show me true
My beautiful, wonderful
Lover new.

After a short while you may see a shadow passing across the mirror—this will be the image of your true love.

To dream of your true love, pick yarrow from the garden of a happily married man and place it under your pillow. Yarrow is a cottage plant that usually has white flowers, growing on tall stalks. It is also believed that upon seeing yarrow for the first time in spring, your wish for love will come true.

Most mediums, spiritualists, and psychics believe that our purpose as souls incarnated on Earth is to discover the true meaning of love. It has even been said that there are but two motivating forces in the human psyche—love and fear—and that every human action is the result of one or the other.

If we were to go through all the ancient and modern manuscripts dealing with spells and magic, the overwhelming number of spells and rituals would likely be concerned with winning the love of another or keeping love alive in a relationship.

Perhaps the reason so many people do not have their fill of love is because they are caught up in a web of its opposite—fear. Fear

can make us jealous, resentful, afraid to show another how we feel in case of rejection, afraid even to love.

Before practicing any of the love spells on the following pages, ask yourself some hard questions. Do you wish to win the love of another because you think you are supposed

to be in love? Do you think that being loved is going to give you your identity?

If you want to enjoy all that love has to offer, begin by saying the following affirmation at least 20 times a day for one week:

I am a magnet for love,
Love is within me,
Without me,
Before me and behind me,
I AM LOVE.

At the end of the week you will find that you feel stronger and more confident of your ability to attract love. Now it is time to get ready to experience the greatest gift the universe can give a human being.

SPELL CRAFT TIP

Love omens

☺ If your lips feel itchy, you will soon receive a kiss.
☺ If your hands shake while writing a love letter, your lover loves you too.
☺ If a dark-haired man unexpectedly kisses you, you will soon receive a marriage proposal.

ATTRACTING A NEW LOVER

This spell is designed to help attract the most suitable person to you. Copper is an important ingredient in love spells, as it is believed to be the metal associated with the goddess of love, Venus.

What do I need?

- Two drops of patchouli essential oil
- A round piece of red leather or silk, approximately 2 in. in diameter
- A small rose quartz crystal (pink), preferably in the shape of a heart
- A copper coin (or round flat piece of copper sheet)
- Approximately 4 in. of copper wire

When should I do this spell?

On a Friday, preferably during the phase of the new moon

What should I do?

Sprinkle the two drops of patchouli oil onto the piece of leather or silk. Place the small rose quartz crystal and the copper coin on the fabric and take up the ends of the cloth to form a small pouch. Use the copper wire to tie the cloth into a pouch.

Hold the pouch in the palm of your hand and allow your body's warmth to heat the oil that has soaked into the fabric. You will soon be able to smell the scent of patchouli.

As you are holding the bag, visualize the type of lover you wish to attract. Be as specific and as graphic as you like. Imagine the image of your new lover being encoded into the copper coin and the quartz.

Carry this bag with you all the time until the next phase of the new moon or until the lover you want appears in your life— whichever comes first.

FINDING A SOUL MATE

A soul mate can be either a very close friend or a lover (or someone who is both). A soul mate is a person who gives you a feeling of being completed. A soul mate can be a person who shares your views, interests, and outlook on life, or a person who complements your personality, a partnership of opposites who share a mutual respect for each other's strengths.

What do I need?
- A tall, narrow candle, preferably white or silver
- Scissors and a sharp knife
- About 12 in. of copper wire
- Matches

When should I do this spell?
Starting on a Friday, preferably during the waxing phase of the moon

What should I do?
This spell takes three days. Break the candle in half. Use your scissors to cut the wick and use a sharp knife to cut away a little of the wax from the wick of the bottom half of the candle.

On the first day, place the candles in the furthest corners of your home. On the second day, place them a little bit closer to each other, but still keep them apart.

On the third day, place the candles side by side in the middle (or heart) of your home. Tie them together with the copper wire, letting the wire spiral evenly around the candles, and light their wicks.

When the candles burn down to the first strand of copper wire, extinguish the flame and watch the smoke—it is rising up to search for your soul mate.

HONORING YOUR RELATIONSHIP: PREPARING A LOVE FEAST

We often forget that food is magical; it absorbs the grower's or cook's emotions. Food that is prepared with love and care will enhance the feeling of nurture and harmony in any social gathering. Kitchen magic is basically being aware of the energy within food and directing that energy toward a particular purpose.

This is a very simple spell. It requires you to add not only certain spices and foods to a meal that you prepare to honor your loved one, but also a feeling of nurture and care. In magical terms, there are a great many foodstuffs that correspond to love (*see also* "Foods of Love" below).

What do I need?
- A rose-colored candle
- Matches
- Your loved one's favorite foods
- A bunch of red flowers, such as roses or carnations
- A shallow bowl
- Two red candles

When should I do this spell?
During the phase of the full moon

What should I do?
Light the candle in the kitchen or near the place where you will do most of your preparation for the meal.

For this meal, use the finest ingredients you can afford and, if possible, cook only with steel, copper, or iron cooking utensils.

As you wash, chop, and mix the ingredients for the meal, focus on giving love and nurture to your loved one. Imagine your loved one eating this food and feeling happy and well cared for.

When using heat to cook the meal, feel it imparting warmth not only to the food but also to the heart of your loved one.

Set the table, again with care and consideration. Place the flowers in the bowl in the center of the table, with the two red candles on either side.

When you are ready to eat, light the candles and say a prayer of thankfulness and protection for your loved one.

FOODS OF LOVE
There countless foods in all sorts of cultures that are believed to be aphrodisiacs, able to enhance the act of making love and to inspire thoughts and feelings of love. They can be offered to a guest you desire, or shared by you and your lover.

Dairy foods
All milk-based products (milk, cream, butter, yogurt, ice cream, cheese) are suffused with the nurturing properties of mothering; milk carries these vibrations.

Fruits

Apricots, apples, pears, peaches, raisins, persimmons, pomegranates, melons, and cherries are filled with the energies of sexual congress, for they are the mode of sexual reproduction for plants. Many people consider the tomato or "love apple" an aphrodisiac.

Vegetables

Because of their phallic shape, cucumbers and asparagus are believed to promote thoughts of love and sex when eaten. The translation of the Aztec name for avocado is "testicle fruit"—eating it was said to heighten a man's sexual drive.

Seafood

Oysters and other shellfish have long been thought of as aphrodisiacs. In myth, the goddess Venus was born of the ocean foam, and her loving energies can be found within the fruits of the sea.

Sweets

Cakes, sugar, honey, cinnamon, nutmeg, allspice, gingerbread, and shortbread are filled with the energies of love. In days of old, cakes were often imbued with love energies and given to desired men or women. Chocolate is said to be full of pheromones or sexual hormones—eating vast amounts of this treat is said to make one fall in love easily.

SPELL CRAFT TIP

Presenting your foods of love

When you are preparing a special meal to invite the energies of love into your life, create the right ambience with a tablecloth and candle in colors of vivid red or pink, with a central flower arrangement of red and yellow roses, jasmine, lavender, honeysuckle, or violets.

LOVE MAGNET SPELL

Spells often work by using ingredients that are sympathetic to the purpose of the spell—thus we use magnets to signify attraction or chewing gum to represent a spell "sticking!"

What do I need?
- A piece of lodestone (or a small magnet)
- An even number of rose petals
- A small feather (preferably pink—if this is not possible, choose any other pretty color except black)
- A small shell (preferably clam shells, conches, or oysters)
- A small, red cloth bag
- Two drops of jasmine or ylang ylang essential oil
- A red piece of heart-shaped paper (you can cut the shape out of a red sheet of craft paper)
- A pen
- A 36 in. length of pink or red embroidery thread

When should I do this spell?
During the phase of the full moon

What should I do?
Put the lodestone or magnet, rose petals, feather, and shell into the cloth bag. Sprinkle the jasmine or ylang ylang essential oil over the ingredients. Put the bag to one side.

On your heart-shaped piece of paper, write down all the qualities you would like your future love to have. Fold the paper up fairly small and tie one end of the embroidery thread around it securely. Sit at a table, or on the floor, with the paper as far away from you as the remaining length of the thread will allow, and with the loose end of the thread close to your hand. Place the bag in front of you.

Pick up the loose end of the thread and slowly pull the paper toward you, imagining your new love being drawn into your life. Say the following words:

I draw my true love unto me,
By power of Earth and Sky and Sea,
By free will and harming none,
You hear my call and soon will come.

Pull the folded paper heart into your bag and use the end of the thread to tie up the bag. Carry or wear the bag with you until your new love appears.

LOVE POWDER SPELL

Love powder can be clandestinely sprinkled on the belongings of a desired person and then in your own underwear drawer to forge a psychic love bond between you. This recipe, from the Caribbean, involves a number of herbs and oils.

What do I need?
• A handful of talcum powder
• Five drops of rose oil
• Five drops of sandalwood oil
• Seven drops of lavender oil
• A teaspoon of powdered cardamom seed
• A teaspoon of powdered allspice
• A teaspoon of crushed and dried lavender
• A teaspoon of crushed and dried rose petals
• A ceramic bowl
• A small jar

When should I do this spell?
Anytime

What should I do?
Combine all the ingredients in the bowl with a fork. As you mix, visualize a warm pink light radiating out from the powder. Gently pour the mixture into the jar. Take the jar with you and sprinkle a little of the mixture on the belongings of a person you desire (and who you know is not indifferent to you). Sprinkle a pinch of the mixture on yourself every day after bathing.

This mixture can also be used to keep a friend or lover thinking about you while he or she is absent. Place a small mound of the mixture on the palm of your hand while standing in a sunny spot

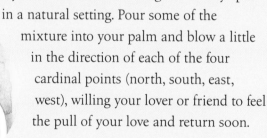

in a natural setting. Pour some of the mixture into your palm and blow a little in the direction of each of the four cardinal points (north, south, east, west), willing your lover or friend to feel the pull of your love and return soon.

LOOKING YOUR BEST

Auras are colors that indicate certain vibrations of energy around you. Some people can see auras around a person's body or head, and judging by how close to the body the color is flaring and what colors are flaring in what areas of the body, they can tell us what emotions we are feeling and what areas are experiencing energy blockages. Use auras to help you feel and look your best for a special occasion.

What do I need?
- A dressing table mirror or full-length mirror that can be tilted so that you can see your head and some space around it
- A piece of glossy paper colored red, green, or purple

When should I do this spell?
Anytime before a special occasion

What should I do?

The first step is to practice seeing your aura. Sit or stand in front of your mirror. If possible, have a dark or white background behind your head.

Stare at the area around your head (the aura in this area is called a nimbus). When your eyes get tired of staring, half close them and see if you can see any shadow or colors around your head.

Usually, if you are nervous, the shadow or color in this area is very close to the head.

Now imagine one of the following colors flaring around your head as a way of invoking the corresponding feeling, not only within yourself, but in the form of energy that will be subconsciously picked up by your date:

purple—calm and control
red—sexy and attractive
green—earthy and stable

Once you feel that you have visualized the appropriate color around your head, cut out a square of paper that corresponds with the color you have chosen and fold it so that it will fit into your pocket, wallet, or purse. Carry the colored paper with you during your date.

LOYALTY SPELL

Here is a spell to encourage loyalty in your friends. In magic there is a belief that like attracts like. If you are a loyal person, you will tend to attract other loyal people. But if you are known to talk about people behind their backs, you may need to correct this tendency before doing this spell.

What do I need?
• One sheet of letter-sized paper
• A black pen
• Scissors
• A small wooden box with a lid
• A single pearl or a pearly opalescent bead
• A pink ribbon

When should I do this spell?
During the phase of the new moon or anytime when you need the help of your friends

What should I do?
Take the sheet of paper and write the word "loyalty" over the entire page, thinking of all the people from whom you seek this kind of support. Turn over the page and write their names in full.

Take the scissors and cut the sheet into long, thin strips of paper. When you have finished, scrunch and roll the strips into a nest that will fit into your box.

Place the paper nest into the box and put the pearl or pearly opalescent bead on top of it. The pearl is symbolic of loyalty. Close the box and tie the ribbon around it.

Hold the box in your hands as you visualize a comfortable cocoon of loyalty being woven around you by the spell. Place the box at a window that gets the morning sun or take it with you when you know you will be facing a crisis.

MAGIC TOOLS AND SPELLS

SPECIAL MAGICAL BROOM SPELL
A magical home usually needs to be cleared of psychic energy as well as scrubbed and dusted. Use the following spell to combine your magical and more mundane housecleaning chores.

What do I need?
- A picture of a beautiful, clean room cut from a magazine
- A small bit of chewing gum or some adhesive tape that is easy to remove
- A broom
- A length of red ribbon

When should I do this spell?
Anytime you need to clean the house

What should I do?
This is a great spell when you have to do cleaning chores around the house. Wrap the picture around the handle of the broom—it may wrap around itself several times. Stick the picture to the handle with the chewing gum or adhesive tape. Then wrap the red ribbon around the picture and tie it in a beautiful bow.

Sweep the house. You will not only be sweeping away the dirt; you will also be sweeping out all the arguments and unhappiness that have occurred since the last time you cleaned the house. Imagine these bad feelings as another kind of grit and grime that needs to be cleared.

Use the broom properly in areas where you usually sweep. Go outside and shake the broom to get rid of the dirt, then go into every room and "sweep" the bad feelings out of each corner of the room. Go outside again and shake out the broom.

Keep the broom by you until you have finished all your cleaning chores. Finish the spell by removing the ribbon and picture from the handle of the broom. Keep the picture, and use it every time you do the cleaning.

MAKING YOUR OWN MAGIC WAND

In spell casting, magic wands are used to help direct your energy into a spell object, such as a pouch of protective herbs or a lucky charm. Magic wands are generally made of wood or metal (often copper).

To get or make a wand, first find a stick that has been thrown to the ground by the wind. Go for a walk through a favorite park, forest or tree-lined street after a windy day, with the specific purpose of finding a suitable branch. Do not pull down a branch that is still connected to a tree—if you do this you are causing harm to the tree and the energy within the branch will be undermined.

Wands traditionally have been made from the wood of the rowan tree or the mountain ash. However, if the branch you find fills the following requirements, use it as your magic wand. The branch should be:
• Fairly straight
• At least 15 in. long
• About half an inch in diameter
• Firm, not diseased or dry
Once you have found the stick that feels right to you, decorate your wand. With marker pens, draw your favorite symbols, such as stars and the moon, or cut the ends so that you can glue a pointed clear quartz crystal at one end and a rounded purple amethyst at the other.

Copper is believed to be an excellent conductor of psychic energy, so wrap some copper wire (you can get it from the hardware store) around the join between the wood and the amethyst then loop the wire up along the stick to the quartz crystal and wrap the wire around that join. You can attach other objects, such as feathers and other beads, to your wand with extra copper wire if you like.

MAKING FRIENDS EASILY SPELL

This spell requires you to gather some magical dew. This will improve your ability to communicate by giving you extra support from Mother Earth and the goddess Moon.

What do I need?
- A silver bowl half-filled with fresh water
- A sprinkle of salt or two drops of magical dew (*see below*)
- A wooden spoon

When should I do this spell?
During the phase of a new or waxing moon

What should I do?
Place the bowl half-filled with water on a low table and sprinkle in the salt or (if you have some) two drops of magical dew. Swirl the water in a clockwise direction with the wooden spoon to mix the salt and dew, feeling the spoon moving easily through the water. Imagine the salt in the water cleansing any bad luck you have had in making friends. Also, think of the easy way the spoon is moving through the bowl of water—this is how easy it will be for you to communicate with people and make friends in the future. When you have finished, throw the water out into the earth, and imagine your spell becoming reality.

SPELL CRAFT TIP
Gathering magical dew drops

At dawn, preferably during summer (particularly on the dawn after Midsummer's Eve, the summer solstice), go outside. Take with you a small jar that has been thoroughly cleaned and dried. Go to each plant that still has dew clinging to its leaves or petals and gently shake some of the dew into your jar. At the end of the day, leave the jar in a window where it will catch the moon's light during the night—the moonlight will infuse the dew with the moon's magical powers. Sprinkle this potion around your room for protection, or add it to other spell ingredients to heighten their magical powers.

MAKING THINGS RIGHT SPELL

When you are in the unfortunate position of having caused someone hurt or harm in an attempt to obtain success for yourself, you must right the situation by undoing some of the damage your actions or behavior inflicted.

The following healing spell will help you commit to unselfishly helping the person you have harmed. There may be a number of ways you can help; you will need to think of what would be suitable in your particular circumstance. By choosing to heal the damage, you will ultimately be able to attract further success in your life.

What do I need?
• A sheet of parchment paper
• Your favorite blue pen
• A small box, preferably made of pine, with a lid
• The dried petals of a pink carnation
• A piece of hematite

When should I do this spell?
On a Sunday

What should I do?
Write at the top of the piece of paper the name of the person you have harmed. On the next line, write down how that person was hurt. On the next several lines, write down all the things you commit to do for that person.

Fold the sheet of paper and place it into the wooden box, along with the pink carnation petals and the hematite. Close the lid of the spell box and place it near your telephone, computer, or in another area in your home where a lot of communication occurs.

The pine box, the carnation petals, and the hematite are excellent symbols of healing, as is the blue ink of your pen. A pink carnation was used because pink represents compassion and friendship.

For the spell to work properly, you must actually do the things you committed to doing. If you don't, you may find yourself in a worse state than you were in to begin with.

MAKING WISHES COME TRUE SPELLS

RUNE FOR MAKING WISHES COME TRUE

Spells for making wishes come true have been popular since ancient times. They focus on a person's ability to bring their wish into reality rather than on the wish itself.

What do I need?

• A flat stone that fits in your pocket

• A black marker pen

When should I do this spell?

Anytime you like

What should I do?

First find your flat stone. Go for a walk that is specially aimed at finding a stone for this spell. Before you leave, imagine that you are searching for a precious stone that will help you obtain all your wishes. If you don't find it the first time you go looking, do not worry; it may take several days to find just the right one. When you find the right stone, draw the rune to the right on it to help your wishes come true.

Keep this stone in your pocket when you are casting any spells.

CANDLE MAGIC FOR MAKING YOUR WISHES COME TRUE

What do I need?

• A red candle

• A pin

• A teaspoon of sunflower oil

• A piece of red fabric big enough to wrap the candle in

When should I do this spell?

During the phase of the new or waxing moon

What should I do?

Engrave your wish along the length of the red candle using the pin. Use as few words as possible when describing your wish. For example, write the words "Money," "Holiday," or "New Job." To get rid of the wax shavings, rub the sunflower oil into the candle, imagining your wish coming true as you rub. Wrap the candle in the red fabric and bury it somewhere outside where it won't be seen; bury it is as close to the front door, gate, or path as possible. The spell is done.

SPELL FOR MAKING WISHES COME TRUE

This is a great spell if there are a number of wishes that you would like to see come true—you can do them all at once!

What do I need?
• A piece of white cardboard
• Some finger paint—about eight or more colors (make sure that your colors include blue and red)
• A mirror big enough for you to see your head and shoulders
• A black marker pen

When should I do this spell?
During the phase of the full moon

What should I do?
In the middle of the piece of cardboard, draw or paint a small picture of yourself. Look at yourself in the mirror and draw and paint what you see.

Use your fingers to paint a blue circle around this picture of yourself, then paint (still with your fingers) eight blue spokes going out from the outside of the circle, like the spokes of a wheel. At the end of each spoke, paint (with your fingers) a smaller blue circle.

Wash your hands and think of the eight things that you would most like to happen in your life. If you have fewer than eight wishes, color in the spare circles with your favorite colors. Do not

have more than eight—your spell will not work.

With your black pen, write or draw a wish in each of the circles you are using. When you have finished, put the piece of cardboard on the floor and walk around it three times. Put the cardboard near where you sleep and check off the wishes as they come true.

MIND POWER AND SPELLS

Spells are powerful ways of focusing your mind so that when you say a particular word, do a certain action, or make a particular object, you set in motion a new course of reality that will allow you to make your wishes come true.

Your mind is a powerful tool. Believing that what you want to happen will happen is one of the most powerful ways in which you can organize and direct your life. Most of us are often assailed by self-doubt, which undermines our ability to make lasting changes in our life. When we learn to focus our minds, we are better able to empower our spells for success.

One of the best ways to focus your mind is to practice visualization. Visualization exercises are easy to do—they simply require a bit of time. Set aside 10 minutes at the same time every day, perhaps near bedtime. Sit on a comfortable chair and think of one object you handled during the day. It can be anything—a two- or three-dimensional object or a picture.

Pick just one object. This in itself is a good exercise, as frequently we are unable to focus on what we want precisely because there are so many things around us clamoring for our attention. The ability to simplify and focus is the key to spell casting, and to gaining success in virtually any other venture in life.

When you have picked an object, focus on it. You have made your choice—now make yourself stick to it. Visualize every detail of the object. Visualize having that object with you again, and try to recreate it so that it appears in a three-dimensional form.

Do this exercise several times before you do any spell craft—improving your visualization skills will give you extra power to fuel and direct your spells.

MIRROR SPELLS

SPECIAL MIRROR SPELL FOR CONFIDENCE

This fun spell will bring you luck, success, and confidence, particularly if you can find a stone called cat's eye, a green quartz crystal that is reputed to bring luck to gamblers, confidence to those suffering depression, and invisibility to those who wear it!

What do I need?

• A mirror with a frame that you can decorate (preferably gold-colored)

• Red, orange, and yellow glass beads and stones

• Two pieces of cat's eye (optional)

• Glue

When should I do this spell?

During the phase of the new or waxing moon

What should I do?

Decorate the frame of the mirror with the beads and stones. These colors are symbolic of the sun and of feelings of success. In the middle of the frame, at the top, glue the two cat's eye stones, if you have them. They will give you a sense of confidence, and will bring you luck with people and money.

A GETTING NOTICED SPELL

This spell combines Eastern and Western philosophies to help you achieve recognition.

What do I need?

• A flat surface where you do your accounts, studies, or work

• A small mirror

• A clear quartz crystal

When should I do this spell?

During the phase of the new or waxing moon

What should I do?

Sit in your chair at your desk as usual and place the mirror and crystal directly opposite where you are sitting. It would be a good idea to place your table lamp in this position as well. According to ancient Chinese beliefs, this area corresponds to fame and acknowledgment. By placing these items in this area of your desk, you will encourage positive energy to help you get noticed!

MONEY AND SPELLS

SEE ALSO **PROSPERITY SPELLS** ON PAGES 148–150.

THE POWER TO ATTRACT PROSPERITY: TRADITIONAL OMENS

Spells for money and wealth often include earthy images, such as objects that are green or brown in color—jade and tiger's eye, for example. One very simple prosperity spell is to light a green candle during the phase of the new or waxing moon. To further empower the spell, look at the candle flame for a moment and then close your eyes, seeing the image of the light in your mind's eye. Shape that light into the image of what you want to purchase with your prosperity.

With any kind of prosperity spells, it is important to be very clear about what you want from the spell. Do you actually want a general sense of prosperity surrounding you or do you want to do something specific with your prosperity? The most successful spells are those that have a very clear and specific purpose.

Over time, a number of interesting and amusing superstitions and omens concerning prosperity have evolved. You will receive some unexpected money if you see a person wearing polka dots, for instance. Certain symbols—a bracelet, catching fish, rain, a calm lake, a full barrel, for example—can also, apparently, presage a prosperous period if they occur frequently in your dreams.

Some physical attributes, such as ears that stick out from the head and the position of any moles on the body, have also been thought to be good omens for prosperity. If you have a mole on your back, you will apparently attract money "by the sack;" a mole on your ear is an indication that you will receive a steady flow of money.

MAKING A MONEY MAGNET

For this spell you can use a naturally occurring magnet (a lodestone) or an artificially charged one, such as the horseshoe magnets you can buy at most hardware stores. Lodestone has been associated with prosperity and money for centuries. Even dreaming of a magnet is thought to indicate that you will earn a lot of money.

What do I need?

- A silver coin or the largest denomination banknote you have at the moment
- A magnet, either a solid circular one or a horseshoe-shaped one
- A large paper clip
- A green silk drawstring bag
- A gold coin, preferably one with a hole in the middle
- A picture of what you wish to purchase with the money (optional)

When should I do this spell?

During the phase of the new moon

What should I do?

Go outside with the silver coin or banknote and hold it up to the moon. Come back inside and put the coin or banknote at one end of a table and the magnet at the other end. Visualize the coin or banknote as the money you desire and the magnet as your desire. As coins often have no iron or not enough iron and banknotes have none, of course, slide the paper clip onto the coin or banknote. Move the magnet slowly toward the money until the money is attracted to the magnet and skips across to it.

As soon as the magnet and money stick together, the spell has begun. Place these two items in the bag, saying the following words:

Maiden Moon, grant me my desire by the time
  you have grown to become a mother.

Say the following words as you put the gold coin into the bag; the coin represents the power of the sun, bringing your wish to life:

Father Sun, grant me my desire before you have grown too old.

The spell is done.

SPELL CRAFT TIP

Coin lore

- ✿ You will have good luck if you pick up a lost coin.
- ✿ Keep any coin that you find during a storm as it is enchanted and will attract good luck to you.
- ✿ Keep a jar of coins in the kitchen to attract prosperity to your household.

MOON AND SPELLS

THE POWER OF THE MOON

The symbol of the new moon, the crescent, was thought to be lucky because it was symbolic of new promise and growth. The phase of the new moon is a perfect time to seek aid and guidance about a new project, business relationship, or career move.

The energy during the new moon is young, wild, strong, and undirected. This is the perfect time to focus your will on what you want to happen in terms of your financial projects or circumstances and to mold a new path for yourself. This is the time to allow your ideas to take seed, no matter how fantastic or ambitious they seem. Anything can happen once you have sown the seeds of your will using new moon energy.

Sometimes knowing which ideas to go with can be difficult; you may wish to seek guidance from the energy of the new moon. On the night of a new moon, write down all your ideas, each on a separate piece of paper. One of the possibilities should always be that you haven't yet identified your best solution.

Find a comfortable space where you can see the moon—it does not matter whether you are outside or inside. Show each piece of paper to the moon then fold it twice, so that you cannot see the writing. Place the folded pieces of paper on the floor at your feet and shuffle them around so that you lose track of which is which.

Concentrate on the moon and her energy. As the energy at new moon time is undirected, use your imagination to mold this energy into a strong, concentrated beam of light that is searching through a myriad of possibilities at your feet. Imagine the beam alighting upon one of the pieces of paper. Pick up the piece of paper and see which path has been chosen.

Before you take any action, do a meditation on the chosen decision. Sit in quiet and clear your head of any extraneous thoughts. Focus your mind on the chosen decision and allow thoughts about the decision to filter into your mind. When you feel ready, emerge from your meditation and write your thoughts down. This is particularly useful if the moonbeam chooses the piece of paper that says you have to think of a new direction. Remember, when you do any work with the moon, you should always thank the moon for her help.

MONEY MAGIC MOON SPELL

At new moon time, empty all the money out of your wallet or purse. Show the money you have in your wallet to the moon,

imagining that as the moon increases or waxes, so too will the amount of money you have. This is a variation on a traditional spell of turning the money in your pocket over the first time you see the new moon.

NEW MOON SPELL

On the day before the new moon's crescent is due, gather some white flowers and put the petals in a bowl of water. Take a moonstone or a clear quartz crystal and place it in the bowl of water as well. When the crescent appears, take out the moonstone or crystal and hold it up to the moon. Say the following words:

Gentle face of Maiden Moon,
Before you I do cast this rune;
As to your fullness you shall grow,
So shall this I wish to know:
That [say what it is you wish].

Put the moonstone or crystal somewhere safe, but show it to the moonlight each of the next three nights, repeating your wish (or question), which should be resolved by the time of the full moon.

PERSONAL ACCEPTANCE SPELL

One of the most powerful forms of magic is the ability to accept who you are and understand fully both your strengths and your weaknesses. The following spell will take you some time to complete. It is an ongoing spell, and its purpose is to remind you that you are worth accepting and loving. The spell involves designing a shrine to your acceptance of yourself.

What do I need?
- A box or wooden structure that can be used as a shrine
- A sheet of paper big enough to cover the back of the shrine
- Gold paint
- Your favorite images or some of your favorite things, such as perfumes, jewelry, or scented candles, that symbolize your taste and what you like
- Your favorite photograph of yourself

When should I do this spell?
Anytime you wish

What should I do?

Take a sheet of paper and draw a small circle in the center, representing you. Paint the circle gold. Then draw a much bigger circle around the first circle, and a number of small circles in the space between the two circles. Each of these small circles represents one of your friends.

Color in these circles with a shade that seems appropriate to each friend and draw a line between each outlying circle and the original circle. Along each line, write in a few words why you think that person is your friend. Do this for each person, eventually creating a mandala (a mystic symbol of the universe) of appreciation of your good qualities.

Attach this sheet to your shrine. Arrange your other favorite images and things in the shrine, perhaps also including a vase of fresh flowers at the front of the shrine.

Keep this shrine in your bedroom, either close to where you sleep or on your dressing table. You may even get a special table to stand the shrine on. Add to your shrine whenever you find an item that specially appeals to you. You may like to also have a small vase nearby in which you can give yourself a small flower each day in appreciation of being who you are.

PERSONAL BEST ACHIEVEMENT SPELL

This spell will help you release any fears about an upcoming game or match and allow you to focus on doing your best.

What do I need?
- A red towel
- A mirror
- A packet of sea salt
- Grass or pebbles from the sports field or the courts where you will be competing

When should I do this spell?

The day before your game or event, finishing it just before you go onto the field or court

What should I do?

In the bathroom or another space where you will not be disturbed, put the red towel on the ground and stand on it, making sure that you can see your face in the mirror. If the space does not have a mirror, bring one.

As you stand on the red towel, lightly sprinkle some sea salt in a circle around you. The red towel symbolizes success—it indicates that you are stepping onto a new path of personal success. The circle of sea salt will protect you from negative energies, including your own doubts and fears.

Sprinkle the grass or pebbles near your feet to anchor the spell to the place where you will be competing. Look at yourself in the mirror and visualize yourself receiving congratulations on achieving your personal best.

Smile and feel a sense of achievement and pleasure in your success. Visualize this feeling being transformed into a golden light that envelops your whole body, traveling from your eyes down to your feet. Bask in the glow, then allow the light to slowly and steadily dissolve into the red towel.

Carefully roll up the towel (without shaking it out) and take it with you to the sports event. Just before the event starts, unroll the towel and shake the salt and grass or pebbles out of it; go out to play feeling that you will achieve your personal best.

PERSONALIZED GOOD LUCK SPELLS

MAKING A PERSONALIZED GOOD LUCK CHARM

A charm was originally a word or phrase that was written down or spoken in a spell. This spell is for a personalized good luck charm that you can put together over a period of time. It will help you generate a positive approach and therefore attract positive energy, improving your luck—remember the phrase "happy go lucky."

What do I need?

- A gold and green drawstring bag, small enough to carry with you (the fabric must be a natural fiber, such as cotton, linen, silk, flax, or hemp)
- A black leather thong (if wearing the bag around your neck)
- Various items that remind you of times when you have been lucky

When should I do this spell?

Anytime you wish

What should I do?

The object of this spell is to collect, over time, personal tokens of occasions when you have been lucky or successful and place them in your gold and green charm bag.

For instance, if you win something in a lottery, put a coin or note from that win into your bag.

Pieces of paper that are an indication of some progress or luck in your work or life can be photocopied (preferably reduced), rolled up into a tight tube, and tied up with a short length of red ribbon. Red is a color that symbolizes success. For instance, photocopy the certificate or diploma awarded to you once you have finished a course, either for work or as part of your academic progress, and put the copy into your bag.

Every time you put a symbol of luck in your bag, say the following words:

Luck for now,

Luck for later.

Keep the bag with you when you want to attract luck or success.

ALL-PURPOSE GOOD LUCK SPELL

Attracting good luck is another area where there are many traditional spells; these take the form of a written word or symbol that can be worn around the neck, or a combination of ingredients that can be worn or imbibed. The spell below pulls together a number of traditional ingredients into a super spell for good luck.

What do I need?

• A green pen

• A purple bag (made of a natural fiber such as silk, cotton, linen, flax, hemp, or leather) big enough to hold the following ingredients:

a business card–sized piece of cardboard

a moonstone bathed in the light of the new moon

four sprigs of lavender

When should I do this spell?

During the phase of the new moon

What should I do?

Before you start the spell, bathe the moonstone in the light of the new moon by holding up the stone so that it covers or partially covers the moon. Take three deep breaths and visualize the moon's rays caressing the stone and imbuing it with lucky qualities.

Draw the outline of a four-leaf clover in the middle of the piece of cardboard, with your green pen. In one leaf write in small letters the word "Fame," in the second leaf, write "Faithful Lover," in the third leaf write "Good Health," and in the fourth leaf write "Wealth."

Draw a circle around the four-leaf clover— this is the simplest and most powerful symbol of protection. Around the circle write your full name, repeating the name as often as it takes to go all the way around the circle.

Put the moonstone, the cardboard, and the sprigs of lavender into the bag.

Your good luck bag can be combined with other images to attract good luck for specific projects and wishes. To direct the energy of good luck to a particular desire, store the good luck bag for three days and nights with a symbol of what you want. If you want a new house or car, for example, store the bag with an image of a house or car.

SPELL CRAFT TIP

Foods of prosperity

Prosperous energies are found in all grains, beans, and seeds, and you can make special magical breads with a few different types of grains, nuts, and herbs under the influence of the planets Mercury, Jupiter, and the sun. Grains and seeds of prosperity include oats, rice, corn or maize, wheat, rye, barley, millet, and sesame seeds.

POPULARITY AND SPELLS

This spell is designed to help you become popular, or at least find one or two good friends, and involves making a simple cloth bag containing some special ingredients that are designed to attract friendship. By making this spell bag, you will be inviting a powerful energy to help you reconnect with the people around you, and to help them see your good qualities.

What do I need?

• The petals of two light pink roses
• A small piece of agate
• A small magnet
• Two drops of patchouli oil
• A square or circle of pink fabric big enough to hold the petals, stone, and magnet
• A length of red ribbon

When should I do this spell?

On a Friday evening

What should I do?

Sit in a quiet place where you will not be disturbed and imagine the room or area you are in bathed in a gentle pink light. Have the ingredients of the spell laid out in front of you. Place the petals, agate, and magnet in the middle of the fabric and measure out the patchouli oil on top of them.

Gather the edges of the cloth and tie up the bag with the red ribbon so that the herbs and magnet are tightly enclosed inside. When the bag is sealed, recite the following words, holding the finished spell bag to your heart.

Let winds of change, by day and night,
Disperse the clouds that hide my light,
And let my soul a beacon be,
To beckon friends and love to me.

—LIAM CYFRIN

Repeat these words over and over again, feeling the energy build up through your body, and raise the bag above your head. When you feel that the energy is about to peak, bring the bag down to the floor, pushing the energy through it and out into the world.

You will need to carry the spell bag with you until you feel that the energy around you at school or work is changing for the better.

EGYPTIAN POPULARITY SPELL

The wish for popularity is as old as the human race. For this popularity spell, we have incorporated a number of ancient Egyptian ingredients. You will even need to inscribe some hieroglyphics!

What do I need?

- A sheet of gold paper (can be a section of wrapping paper)
- A black marker pen
- A red ribbon
- A small piece of yellow or gold cloth
- A needle
- Some yellow or gold thread
- A length of silk cord
- Two of each of the following semiprecious stones:
  carnelian, lapis lazuli, hematite

When should I do this spell?

During the phase of the full moon

What should I do?

Tear a strip measuring about 6 in. long and about 2 in. wide from the gold paper. The gold color symbolizes the power of the sun, and has powerful attractive energies. The sun helps bring to light a person's best qualities. Along the length of the strip of paper, draw the following hieroglyphics:

Although it is best to draw these symbols yourself, if you find it too difficult, photocopy them, cut the copy out, and stick it onto your paper. These hieroglyphics spell out the word "Popularity."

Roll up the strip of paper tightly so that the hieroglyphics are on the inside. Tie the red ribbon around the roll of paper to secure it. Make your cloth into a narrow bag that the gold roll will fit into. When you have slipped the roll into the bag, sew a line of running stitch and draw the thread through the fabric so that the top edge gathers together to enclose the roll. Sew a few stitches to secure the gathers.

To wear this around your neck, tie a length of silk cord around the top of the bag so that the bag hangs from the middle of the cord. Thread three stones on each side of the bag and tie a knot after the stones to keep them in place. Then you can tie the ends of the silk cord behind your neck and wear the bag and stones until you feel that you are becoming more popular.

POTIONS AND SPELLS

POTENT LOVE POTIONS

Potions have been brewed since ancient times for various magical purposes. This form of magic was linked closely with the psychic properties of various herbs. Not surprisingly, most of the potions concerned attracting love.

Ingredients of love potions included warming spices, such as cinnamon, cloves, and even pepper, and the roots of various plants, such as ginseng and St. John's Wort (otherwise known as "John the Conqueror"). One of the most potent ingredients in a love potion was the legendary satyrion root (trifolium), which is mentioned in a number of ancient texts.

There appears to be no modern equivalent of the satyrion, which had a bifurcated root. The lower part of the root was thought to be beneficial for reviving a male's flagging interest, and the upper part was usually used to help women become pregnant. If the satyrion root was dissolved in goat's milk, the potion was guaranteed to make the drinker almost insatiable. Sometimes the root of a particular orchid is labeled as satyrion root, but it is not exactly the same.

Mandrake was another root that has been used in love potions throughout the ages. It was described by the ancient Greek physician Dioscorides in his Materia Medica as an excellent stimulant, especially when steeped in wine. Often taking the shape of a man, mandrake root came to be called Aphrodite, after the Greek goddess of love. Dioscorides also names other ingredients for love potions, including *cardamon lepidium sativum* (cynocardamom), and even the humble turnip.

Not all love potions were taken internally. Sometimes ingredients were gathered into a small bag and placed under a person's pillow to attract love to them, and sometimes the ingredients would be ground and then blown in the face of the person the spell caster wished to attract.

A MAGICAL POTION TO BRING PEACE TO A TROUBLED HOME

If your family or roommates have been going through a difficult time, which has been manifesting as an overflow of anger and frustration, you will need to clear the air—an accumulation of this negative energy can cause serious rifts and even physical damage. Try the following spell to create a much more peaceful space in your home.

What do I need?
• Lavender water or 10 drops of lavender essential oil
• An atomizer bottle filled with filtered water, 16 fl. oz.
• A small silver ring
• A piece of chlorite or citrine (optional)

When should I do this spell?
When arguments flare up or during the phase of the waning moon

What should I do?
First, assess which areas need clearing. The kitchen is often one of the main areas where disputes occur—there is a great deal of fiery energy being generated by the stove, oven, microwave, and other cooking appliances.

Measure out 10 drops of lavender water (or essential oil) into the filtered water and drop the silver ring into the atomizer bottle. The shape of a ring—a circle—is a symbol of protection, and silver invokes the power of the moon.

If you are able to find one, place a piece of chlorine in the water; it helps eliminate hostility and anger. Alternatively, you could include a piece of citrine, reputed to help with problem solving.

Go to each room where arguments have flared up and clap vigorously in each corner, dislodging the negativity residing there. When you feel ready, zap the negative energy with a few sprays from the atomizer. Imagine the energy harmlessly dispersing. The spell has worked if the room feels lighter and looks brighter. Take the ring out of the water once you have finished clearing your home, and wear it until the issues are fully resolved.

PROSPERITY SPELLS

PROSPERITY OIL SPELL

Prosperity formulas usually use herbs thought to be under the influence of Jupiter, the planet of bounty and abundance. This classic prosperity oil has been used for at least one hundred years by the Hoodoos, followers of the magical tradition of New Orleans.

What do I need?
- A dark glass jar with a lid
- Six parts base oil (virgin olive, sunflower, or light mineral)
- One part basil powder
- One part spearmint essential oil
- One quarter part cinnamon essence
- Some cheesecloth to strain the mixture
- A pouring jug
- A small coin

When should I do this spell?
The oil is traditionally compounded on a Thursday, the sacred day of the planet Jupiter, and is believed to be most effective if allowed to sit for three weeks after being mixed

What should I do?
Gather your ingredients and find a cool dark place you can concoct this potion in. Pour the base oil into the dark glass jar, then add the basil powder, spearmint oil, and cinnamon essence. Mix the ingredients well. Put the lid on the jar and leave the mixture to sit for at least three weeks. If you want to make a mixture to use in your aromatherapy oil burner, combine just the basil powder, spearmint oil, and cinnamon esssence.

Strain the mixture through cheesecloth or muslin into a pouring jug to remove the basil powder residue. Then wash and dry the jar, place the coin in it, and pour the mixture back in. Put the lid on the jar and store it away from the rays of the sun.

Rub a tiny drop of the oil onto your bank statements and checkbooks, contracts, and share certificates to draw wealth to you. Or you could measure a drop or two of the oil onto a small piece of green cloth and keep the cloth in your purse or wallet.

The oil may be worn as a perfume. Use less cinnamon oil than is listed above if you are making perfume to be worn on your skin— cinnamon essential oil may burn.

CORNUCOPIA POWDER SPELL

Sprinkle this powder over your head and around your home when you need a change of fortune. Carry some in a little, yellow paper envelope to meetings and interviews—this is said to draw the energies of success to you.

What do I need?
- A small glass jar (with a lid) for mixing the Cornucopia Powder
- A glass jar large enough to hold an apple
- One-eighth part citronella essential oil
- One part basil powder
- One part spearmint powder
- One part aniseed powder
- One-half part nutmeg powder
- Five parts talcum powder
- A tiny piece of paper
- A pen
- An apple and apple corer
- White sugar
- White wine

When should I do this spell?
On a Thursday on or after a new moon

What should I do?
Mix the basil, spearmint, aniseed, nutmeg, talcum power, and citronella in the small jar—this is your Cornucopia Powder.

Next, write a brief description of your goal or aim on a tiny piece of paper and roll the paper into a miniature scroll. Using an apple corer, bore a hole halfway into the apple. Keep the "plug" of apple you remove. Place the scroll in the hole, add a sprinkling of

Cornucopia Powder, and replace the apple "plug." Place the apple in a jar and cover it completely with white sugar and white wine. Put the lid on the jar and pray for success. Put the jar beneath your bed or in your bedside cabinet. As the apple, sugar, and wine ferment, so too does the energy of your goal.

PROTECTION AND SPELLS

Some spell casters believe that ignoble human motives such as spite, envy, and hatred are the results of the intervention of negative energies—many spells have been created to absorb, destroy, ward off, and cast out these energies.

Many people also believe that some individuals are born with the evil eye, the ability to destroy the joy of others with nothing more than a passing glance. A person with the evil eye is believed to be possessed by the spirit of envy, and even a fleeting look can sink a boat at sea, sour milk, render breeding stock infertile, and cause a crop to wither and perish. Many people in southern Europe believe in the evil eye, and all kinds of charms may be found in Italy and Greece to ward off this menace.

Traditional charms against the evil eye include a tiny horn carried in the pocket, a glass eye or a single blue bead worn on a chain around the neck, and even a "figa" hand signal (a closed fist with the thumb thrust between the index and middle fingers). Little figa hands are often made in gold or silver and worn around the neck. Images of blue and white eyes are incorporated into jewelry, painted on houses and boats, and molded into brass charms to be hung on the bridles of horses. These charms are believed to draw the gaze of the evil eye away from the target and toward the charm.

There are also magical powders, oils, and charms that can be worn or carried to protect against vampires. In magic, the term vampire refers to an often unwitting person who drains the psychic energy from people, leaving them depressed, worn, even sickly. Such people seem to suck the life force out of a room or person and use it to bolster their own energy levels. There are many ways people practicing spell craft can protect themselves against this.

MISCELLANEOUS PROTECTION CHARMS

There are countless little charms and amulets used to protect yourself and your property against harm. Here are some of the more effective ones:

- Mistletoe, also known as golden bough, carried in a small hand-sewn cloth bag is a traditional Celtic method of personal protection; it is also used by followers of the magic in the South.
- Marjoram or wild oregano is believed to absorb dangerous negative energies when it is powdered and sprinkled around the home. Followers of Italian witchcraft (stregeria) make this herb into a tea and add it to the wash and scrub water to protect the home and its inhabitants.
- Cuban and Puerto Rican followers of the folk religion, known as Santería, regularly burn brown sugar, a pinch of sulphur, and garlic powder on charcoal inside their homes to cleanse the home of any negative energy. When the home has been cleansed it is protected by praying to Santa Barbara, the saint of protection, by the light of a red and a white candle.
- A pinch of sulphur powder and cayenne pepper carried in a small, brown paper pouch that has a sword drawn on it can be carried to ward off hostile words and deeds.
- In the magic of the South, plain bluing powder (used to whiten clothes in the wash) is said to ward off evil spirits. The bluing powder is generally carried in a small blue paper pouch.
- A tiny silver bell worn about the neck is a very potent protective charm, because evil spirits cannot abide the sweet ring of any bell.
- Mirrors are said to frighten away dark spirits; this is why tiny pieces of silvered glass are often sewn into Indian cotton dresses. So are bells, for the same purpose.

PERSONAL PROTECTION SPELL

The following spell is based on the magical power of names. You can use your given name or create a magical name for yourself.

What do I need?

- Clay that sets when fired in an ordinary oven (all white or half white and half red)
- A pin
- Pieces of drilled red coral (if possible) or red paint

- A fine paintbrush
- Black paint
- A length of black silk thread
- Some hematite beads (optional)

When should I do this spell?
During the phase of the full moon

What should I do?
Fashion half your clay (use white clay for this) into small, square beads about ¼ in. wide. Stick a pin through the center of each bead and widen the hole until the thread will easily fit through it. Make the hole larger than you need to, because clay usually shrinks during the firing process.

If you have pieces of drilled red coral, skip the following step of the spell, which is to make pieces of coral-looking beads. Shape the other half of your clay (the red half if you have red) into small, bulbous, irregular shapes and stick the pin into each shape a number of times to make it look like coral. Coral is an excellent "stone" of protection.

Also, stick the pin all the way through the beads (as you did with the square beads) so that they can be strung. Put the beads and the coral shapes into the oven and follow the manufacturer's instructions to fire them.

Once they have cooled, paint your name on the square beads—one letter per bead—using the paintbrush and the black paint; paint the "coral" beads red, if necessary, as well.

Using the silk thread, string the letters of your given or magical name with the coral shapes and the hematite beads (if you have them), using at least one coral shape between each two letters of your name. Hematite has traditionally been used to ground the magic of the spell into reality; it makes sure that you will feel the protection of the spell in the real world.

A MEXICAN CHARM BAG FOR PROTECTION

Mojo or charm bags are used for many magical purposes in Mexico. The following charm bag is used to protect against all harm. It is made in honor of the Mexican saint of protection, Santa Marta.

What do I need?
- A small square of vivid red cloth
- A pinch of white pepper
- A portion of sage

- A sprinkling of powdered garlic
- A dash of cayenne pepper
- A sprinkling of tobacco
- A thorn from a cactus or rose
- A small tiger's eye or cat's eye stone
- Red thread
- Scissors
- A needle
- A red candle in a stable candleholder
- Matches

When should I do this spell?

Anytime you wish, or during the phase of the full moon

What should I do?

Take the square of red cloth and fold it in half to create a rectangle large enough to be sewn into a small bag suitable for carrying in your purse or wallet, or in your pocket.

Place the pepper, sage, garlic, cayenne pepper, and tobacco, plus the thorn and the tiger's eye or cat's eye in a little mound on one half of the rectangle of cloth and fold the other side of the cloth over it to encase the contents. Carefully sew around the edges of the cloth, being careful to keep all the contents within the bag.

Kiss the charm, place it beneath your pillow, and sleep on it for four consecutive nights. On the fifth night, sit in a quiet space where you will not be disturbed. Have matches and a red candle in a stable candleholder in front of you and the charm bag in your hands. Close your eyes and visualize brilliant red energy emanating from the charm bag, growing stronger and radiating out to fill the room. Light the candle and recite the following prayer to Santa Marta:

Sanctified Santa Marta, bless and cleanse me of my woes.
Slay the dragon of my misfortune and light my way upon the path
To peace and tranquillity. Bless my charm and occasion it to
Protect me against all harm in your name.

Carry the charm on your person from then on.

R

RECORDING YOUR SPELLS

STARTING YOUR OWN SPELL JOURNAL

Consider starting your own spell journal to keep all your ideas and information about spells, seasonal celebrations, and other rituals you are interested in using in one place. The journal can be anything from an ordinary exercise book to a handmade book of recycled or rice paper.

You may want to use a ring binder so that when you have more information on a particular type of magic, you can simply add an extra page in the appropriate place, keeping all the spells in one category together. Try to find a book or binder that you can lock, or keep your journal in a specially made bag so that no one can look at your work.

Your spell journal is a very private book. Include information about the results of your spells, taking particular note of any vivid dreams that you may have the night after you have cast a spell. Keep your journal beside your bed and write down any dreams that you remember as soon as you wake up.

Dreams are particularly useful in giving you insight about your life and your magic work. Examining the dreams you have after performing spells and other magic work can also help strengthen your intuition.

When you write down a special spell or ritual that you would like to try, leave a couple of pages to make a note of exactly how you performed the spell. When you do the spell or ritual, write down as many details as possible of what you were feeling when preparing and doing it, what your ingredients were and how you prepared them, when you did the spell or ritual, and whether or not you noticed any particularly unusual or curious events after the spell was cast or the ritual was performed.

THE KEY OF SOLOMON THE KING (CLAVICULA SALOMONIS)

King Solomon is reputed to have been the legendary author of this grimoire or magic journal. The grimoire's fame predominantly stems from the fact that it contains instructions on how to summon and control various spirits to do the bidding of the King.

Another text, *The Testament of Solomon*, tells a story of the King deriving his power over the spirits or demons from a ring that was given to him by an angel sent by God. There are other spells in the grimoire or in the *Testament* that were designed specifically to bring death and destruction to another person.

However, the importance of the work is immeasurable. There are numerous versions of *The Key of Solomon the King*. Samuel Liddell Mathers' 1888 English translation attempted to marry several versions (all held at the British Museum), including a late sixteenth century version. In his translation, Mathers was careful to exclude those spells that could be classified as "black magic," warning that if a person wants "to work evil, be assured that that evil will recoil on himself and that he will be struck by the reflex current."

SPELL CRAFT TIP

Making a magic carpet according to
The Key of Solomon the King

"Make a carpet of white and new wool, and when the moon shall be at her full, in the sign of Capricorn and in the hour of the sun, thou shalt go into the country away from any habitation of man, in a place free from all impurity, and shalt spread out thy carpet so that one of its points shall be toward the east, and another toward the west, and having made a circle without it and enclosing it, thou shalt remain within upon the point toward the east, and holding thy wand in the air for every operation, thou shalt call upon Michael, toward the north upon Raphael, toward the west upon Gabriel, and toward the south upon Uriel."

REVIVING RELATIONSHIP SPELLS

REVIVING A LUSTERLESS RELATIONSHIP

The following spell is based on the concept of sympathetic magic—
by polishing up a metal frame you are symbolically also polishing
up your romance.

What do I need?

- A decorative metal picture frame
- Tarnish remover or a reliable, gentle polish
- A soft cloth
- A picture of the two of you during your time of courtship or
  when you first got together
- A white candle in a metal candleholder
- Matches

When should I do this spell?

Start during the phase of the new moon

What should I do?

Find a metal picture frame that will suit your photograph. Polish
the frame and fit the photograph into it. Place it in a prominent,
high position in the space you and your partner share, such as on
the mantelpiece, a dresser, or an upper shelf of a bookcase.

Place the candle, in its stand, on the left-hand side of the picture
frame (as you look at it). The left-hand side represents the intuitive
and magical side of life. Light the candle and say the following
words:

Let us feel our love revive,

So that our passion may survive.

While the candle is burning, take some time to visualize your love
deepening and strengthening. Let your mind go blank and let any
thoughts about how to do this come through. Do not be distressed
if some old anger or disappointment surfaces.

This is an indication that this issue is
somehow interfering with the revival
of passion and sense of
connection that you seek with
your partner.

Every three days, clean and
polish the frame and the
candleholder with the cloth—this
cloth should be used only for this

purpose—and light the candle. Say the words above and take a few moments to visualize your relationship reviving. Do this spell over a 30-day period. When this period is over, remove the candle, but leave the picture in its honored position in your home together. You will be amazed at the results!

REVIVING A SENSE OF GOODWILL AND RESPECT
Generosity and goodwill are important factors in a happy, long-lasting relationship. If you are in a tense relationship, try simply changing the flow of energy in the relationship from negative to positive by focusing on finding and appreciating aspects of your partner's or friend's character that you respect.

Try to honor these character traits for three days and nights and see if there is a shift in the person's behavior toward you. This is often all that is needed to change the dynamics of a relationship for the better. If you feel too angry to do this, try the following spell.

What do I need?
• A silver bowl full of water
• A small rose quartz crystal ball

When should I do this spell?
During the phase of the new moon

What should I do?
The silver bowl full of water used in this spell is symbolic of the nurturing energy of the moon. Sit in a special place (either inside or outside) in view of the new moon and gaze into the bowl of water, visualizing yourself bathing in the water, washing away all your anger and frustration about the relationship.

When you feel ready, pick up your ball of rose quartz crystal and cleanse it in the bowl of water. Enjoy the sensation of the water gliding over the smooth, rounded stone. Visualize generosity and goodwill coming back into your relationship as easily as the water is gliding over the crystal ball.

Pour the water into the earth and keep the stone beside you whenever you are communicating with your partner or friend.

SAFE TRAVEL SPELLS

A SPELL FOR SAFETY WHILE TRAVELING

This spell involves drawing a powerful talisman and pasting it onto
the cover of a small travel journal that you take with you on your
journey.

What do I need?

- A hardcover travel journal (pocket-sized if possible)
- A picture of yourself (or someone else if you don't have one of
  yourself) during a previous happy holiday or a successful and safe
  business trip
- A black pen
- A circular piece of white or silver cardboard that fits onto the
  cover of the journal
- Glue or double-sided adhesive tape

When should I do this spell?

On the Monday before you travel, at dawn, so you can tap into the
psychic protection of the moon

What should I do?

Draw the following talismanic design on one
side of the white or silver cardboard:

On the other side of the cardboard write the
following words:

Journey safely in body, mind, and soul

The cardboard talisman should then be pasted or taped onto the
front of your travel journal, with the talismanic design visible and
the words facing the cover.

Open the journal and make an itinerary for each day you will be
away, using one page per day. If you wish, you can actually use the
journal to plan or map out your journey. On each page, write the
words above.

If you are going on a business trip, you can help ensure financial
success by carrying your travel journal—and a piece of bloodstone
—in a black drawstring bag. This stone is excellent for inspiring

courage under pressure and attracting wealth. It is also excellent for preventing theft, and dispels negative energy directed toward you by competitors or enemies.

A SPELL FOR SAFETY IN WORLD TRAVEL

This spell is another method of protecting a traveler while he or she is away from home. Do this spell for yourself or on behalf of a loved one (make sure you have their permission).

What do I need?

- An orange candle
- A length of fine copper wire as long as your arm
- A stick of lavender, sandalwood, or lemongrass incense
- Matches
- A neck chain or a length of leather thong
- A blue bead with a hole through it that is large enough to thread the chain or leather strip through
- Lemongrass essential oil (optional)

When should I do this spell?

On a Wednesday, early in the morning—at dawn if possible

What should I do?

Place all the items you need for the spell neatly in front of you. Coil the copper wire around the candle from the base to the tip, in a spiral. Light the candle and the incense stick. Thread the chain (or leather) through the bead—this will become an amulet worn by the traveler—and hold the two in your hand. Recite the following:

> *Little King Mercury, swift and alert, be on guard here and*
> *Watch ever vigilantly for me [or name of traveler].*
> *Bless this amulet made in your name and let it be*
> *A stout and true guard against all malady, hurt, fear, trial, and*
> *tribulation.*

Breathe on the amulet seventeen times, with your eyes closed, and feel the energy of your breath grow stronger and more potent with each breath. Try to push this energy into the amulet. If you wish to, you can anoint the amulet with lemongrass essential oil before you wear it (or give it to the traveler you have made it for).

SAYING GOODBYE SPELL

We all go through unhappy times when we have to say goodbye to
a friend, relative, or partner who has passed away. The pain of loss
is almost unbearable at first. There is no spell that can truly
eliminate that feeling of loss. However, the following spell may help
you say goodbye with honor and dignity.

What do I need?
- A picture of the person who has passed away
- A sprig of rosemary
- An object that they gave you out of love
- A white candle
- A fragrance that reminds you of your friend, relative, or partner,
  or lavender essential oil
- A stable candleholder
- Matches

When should I do this spell?
Within three weeks of the person's death

What should I do?
Assemble your ingredients and tools on a shelf or other spot where
the arrangement won't be disturbed. Set up the picture of the
person and place the rosemary and the person's gift to you in front
of the picture.

Wipe the candle with the fragrance or lavender oil, place it in the
candleholder and position it behind the picture. When you are
ready, light the candle and pick up the treasured gift.

Feel the person's energy with you, and
feel the link between you. Use this
feeling to say your goodbye to
them and to wish them safe
passage. Take this opportunity to
feel their soothing presence with
you; feel them comforting you.

When you feel ready,
extinguish the candle. Use this
spell whenever you feel the need
to be comforted.

SPACE PROTECTION SPELL

This spell involves creating an ancient symbol of protection—that of the eye. This will help you protect your personal space.

What do I need?

- Fabric (such as cotton or heavy-duty calico) that is as long as the width of the door to your bedroom and as wide as you like, to make into a flag or a banner (make sure that it is at least as wide as your hand is long)
- A length of white fringing
- A black marker pen
- Colorful fabrics, beads, sequins, ribbons (optional)

When should I do this spell?

During the phase of the full moon

What should I do?

Cut out the fabric so that it extends right across your door. In the middle of the fabric draw a large eye. You can use the Egyptian style "Eye of Horus" (*right*) or you can just draw a simple almond shape with a circle in the middle.

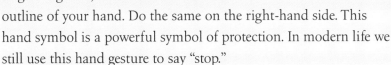

On the left-hand side of the image of the eye, place your hand, palm down and fingers together, on the fabric. Draw the outline of your hand. Do the same on the right-hand side. This hand symbol is a powerful symbol of protection. In modern life we still use this hand gesture to say "stop."

Attach the white fringing to the bottom of the banner or flag, the side that will be hanging down over the door. The fringe represents a filtering of energy—the negative energy will be kept out and the positive energy will be allowed into your room.

If you wish, you may decorate the banner with any beads, sequins, ribbons, and other colorful fabrics, maybe stitching a length of different colored ribbons over the outline of your hands and the eye symbol. Now hang this banner or flag over the door (on the inside of your room or outside in the hall).

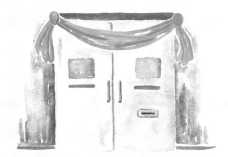

SPECIAL LEARNING AND RECALL SPELLS

SPECIAL LEARNING SPELL

When your mind feels cluttered and tired, it feels as if there is no way you can cram yet another fact into it. This spell uses coffee beans, incense, a semiprecious stone that resonates with clarity of mind, and a simple action that you can do with your arms to stimulate your thinking processes.

What do I need?

- A stick of frankincense incense and an incense holder
- Matches
- Two coffee beans
- Two pieces of clear quartz crystals (both should have a naturally occurring point, ideally) that fit comfortably in your hand
- A silver bowl

When should I do this spell?

In the evening, whenever you feel tired but need to go on

What should I do?

Stand in a place where you will not be disturbed and where you can see the glow of the moon. Place the incense stick in its holder on the ground or floor about 3 ft. away from you. Light it and stand back in your original position, holding a coffee bean and a clear quartz crystal in each hand.

Using large actions, hold your hands up and apart, as if you are reaching to the moon. Spread your legs out so that you are basically the shape of an "X." In this spell, the cross is a symbol that protects against unclear thinking.

Move your arms across your body so that your left hand is pointing to the right and your right hand is pointing to the left. Uncross your arms, taking them back to the original position,. and repeat this crossing and uncrossing action eight more times (do it nine times in total).

Place the crystals and the coffee beans in a silver bowl, and put the bowl on your desk near textbooks that seem particularly difficult to learn from or other material you are having difficulty mastering.

SPECIAL RECALL SPELL

The following spell for improving your memory under stress is based on invoking the powers of the four elements—Air, Fire, Water, and Earth. This is a spell that you can tap into during the exam without drawing attention to yourself.

What do I need?

• Four colored pencils—light blue, red, turquoise (blue-green), brown
• Short lengths of narrow light blue, red, turquoise, and brown ribbon
• Four sprigs of rosemary
• Magnetite stone or necklace (optional)

When should I do this spell?

The night before the exam and during the exam

What should I do?

On the night before the exam, tie a colored ribbon around each sprig of rosemary. These ribbons and pencils correspond to the four elements of the universe—Air (light blue), Fire (red), Water (turquoise), and Earth (brown).

Pick up the rosemary tied with light blue ribbon and the light blue pencil. Hold the pencil and rosemary together and visualize the power of Air emanating from the pencil and herb. Air corresponds to intelligence. Pick up the rosemary tied with red ribbon and the red pencil, and imagine the power of Fire, which corresponds to being creative.

Continue with turquoise and imagine the power of Water, of having your emotions and fears contained. End with brown and imagine the power of Earth, of being practical and grounded in your approach to the exam.

Pack the bundles of herb and the pencils into your school bag or briefcase. On the day of the exam, wear your magnetite necklace or carry the stone in your pocket. This stone has a particular energy that will enhance your ability to recall what you have studied.

Take the pencils into the exam and leave the rosemary in your bag. If you are having difficulty remembering the information, hold the four colored pencils in your hand— you will recall the information you need.

STAYING TRUE TO YOURSELF SPELL

Never be tempted to be something or someone you are not.
Staying true to yourself is one of the most fundamental tools to
having lasting, loving relationships. Being loved for who you are is
much more satisfying than molding yourself to what someone else
wants you to be. Try to resist this type of manipulation. The
following spell will help you gain a true sense of who you are—and
keep it while you are out with your friends or your date.

What do I need?
• A lock of your hair
• Some of your nail clippings
• A passport-sized picture of yourself smiling
• A royal blue–colored cloth bag big enough to contain the
  hair, nail clippings, picture, piece of paper,
  and seeds
• A favorite pen
• A small piece of paper (about 7–10 in.)
• Eight sunflower seeds still in their
  shells
• A piece of black leather thong or thin
  ribbon

When should I do this spell?
Anytime before an outing or a date

What should I do?
Put the lock of your hair, your nail clippings, and your photograph
into the cloth bag. Sit comfortably in your favorite room, chair, or
space. Put the little bag in your lap.

With your favorite pen, write down the positive qualities that
define who you are on the sheet of paper (such as good-humored,
optimistic, lively, thoughtful). Also write down what you like and
dislike generally and in a relationship. Take some time and put
together a really good list.

When you are sure the list is complete, fold the paper and place
it in the blue bag. Pour in the sunflower seeds and tie the bag with
the leather thong or silk ribbon.

Carry the bag with you to the date to remind you of your worth
and that you should not lose sight of who you truly are.

STOPPING THE INTERRUPTIONS SPELL

Try the following spell if you are suffering constant interruptions. It uses faceted lead crystal glass to help deflect unnecessary disturbances.

What do I need?

• A faceted lead (artificial) crystal for each opening in your bedroom or study

• A bundle of dill tied with red ribbon for each opening in your bedroom or study and for the back of your chair

• Push pins

• A small hand mirror, preferably on a stand (optional)

When should I do this spell?

During the phase of the full moon or whenever you get too many interruptions during an important period of study

What should I do?

Gather the crystals and your tied bundles of dill. You don't have to wash the "crystal," because it is not naturally occurring, and because in this spell it is used only to deflect, not to store, energy.

Sit at your desk and visualize a blue haze emerging from the Earth and seeping up through the floorboards around the edges of your room. The blue light symbolizes protective energy—it will protect you against negative, unharmonious, and time-wasting energy.

Hang a bundle of dill and a faceted lead crystal over each opening to your bedroom or study, using the push pins. Also hang a bundle of dill from the back of your chair. Dill is used in magic to protect, and to help clear the mind and aid logical thinking.

If, when you are studying, your back faces the door, place a mirror in front of you on your desk so that you can see a reflection of the door—or rearrange your study so that you are facing the door. In feng shui, sitting with your back to a door is believed to lead to your suffering disruptions.

When you have finished your studying or work, make sure you visualize the blue light going back down into the ground—if you forget to do this, you may find that you get no visitors!

STRENGTHENING YOUR WILL SPELL

Having the willpower to complete a project or do something that you don't really want to do but is good for you can be difficult if you are not fully focused on the task. The following spell will help you strengthen your willpower for whatever purpose you desire.

What do I need?
• A piece of red agate or a red marble
• A piece of paper
• A red pen
• A piece of red string

When should I do this spell?
Anytime, or during the phase of the new moon

What should I do?
Hold the red stone or marble in your hand (your left hand if you write with your right hand, your right hand if you write with your left hand). The red color corresponds to the element of Fire, which is symbolic of your will. Squeeze as hard as you can and feel that your will is as strong as the stone or marble.

With your other hand, write the following words nine times on the piece of paper with your red pen:

I wish to have the willpower to [insert what you want to do or finish].

Roll up the piece of paper as tightly as you can and tie it with the red string. Place the rolled paper with the stone or marble somewhere in your room where the noon sun reaches.

This is when our most powerful naturally occurring energy—the sun—achieves its full strength.

Leave the items there for three days. You will soon find that you will be able to achieve your goals.

STRESS RELEASE SPELL

We are continually subjected to stress. There are a number of effective ways of releasing stress magically, particularly by using the powers of the full moon.

What do I need?

- A silver-colored bowl full of spring or filtered water (a bowl made of stainless steel, for instance)
- A piece of clear quartz crystal (choose a piece that is pleasantly smooth to your touch)

When should I do this spell?

In the evening during the phase of the full moon

What should I do?

This exercise must be done under the light of a full moon. Do this exercise outside, or with the window open in a space where you won't be disturbed and where the moon's rays are shining onto your spell-casting area.

Make sure your bowl is washed and polished. Wash your stone under running water to remove any previous energy.

When you are ready, place your bowl of water on the moonlit floor or ground. Hold the stone so that it catches the light of the moon. Next, hold the stone in the bowl of water and allow the water to flow over it as if you were washing away all the feelings of stress from your body into the water. Imagine the water and the moon's rays cleansing the stress out of the stone.

Continue doing this until you feel calm and relaxed. Dry your stone and pour the water into the earth. Sit awhile, holding your stone, enjoying a release from your worries. Carry the stone with you during the day and rub it when you begin to feel any stress again. The moon's power, now contained in the stone, will help relieve your anxiety.

TALISMANS AND SPELLS

WHAT ARE TALISMANS?

Many powerful talismans were outlined in one of the world's most famous grimoire or magic textbook—*The Key of Solomon the King*. It is one of the oldest magical texts known to humankind, and was widely believed to have been written by King Solomon himself, who had the reputation of being a master magician.

Talismans also feature in other grimoires and magic textbooks. In all these sources, a talisman is an object imbued with special power to attract or repel certain energies, and can be made to attract protection, love, health, or financial success to its wearer.

To permeate a simple metal talisman with magical powers to help or protect its owner, make the talisman using a certain set of sigils or numbers, and make it on the day of the week to attract the

type of energy you need. In the old texts, each day of the week corresponded with one of seven major celestial bodies identified at that time—the sun, moon, Mercury, Venus, Mars, Jupiter, and Saturn. Each celestial body had a corresponding magical energy. For a discussion of corresponding celestial energy, see page 46. See also page 14 for spells that

CELESTIAL BODY	DAY	CORRESPONDING MAGICAL ENERGY
Sun	Sunday	wealth, fortune, friendships
Moon	Monday	diplomatic missions, reconciliation, psychic ability
Mercury	Wednesday	eloquence, intelligence, business partnerships, protection against theft
Venus	Friday	love, travel, friendships
Mars	Tuesday	honor, courage, protection
Jupiter	Thursday	acquiring riches, new friendships, preserving health
Saturn	Saturday	business success, acquisition of learning, luck

correspond to the seven celestial bodies; page 46 for associated colors, metals, stones, or resins; and pages 102–103 for corresponding herbs.

Making the talisman on a particular day and making it of a metal that corresponds to the appropriate celestial body, as well as using the appropriate symbols, words (sometimes in Hebrew) or numbers, would imbue it with a delicate vibration that would magically attract the appropriate protection or help to the wearer.

A TALISMAN FOR PROTECTION

The particular design and method of use for this talisman of protection are adapted from *The Key of Solomon the King*. Magical practitioners have used this talisman for centuries as protection against all kinds of negative forces. The design is said to be the most perfect double acrostic in existence—the words can be read on any horizontal or vertical plane.

What do I need?
- A piece of black card small enough to fit into a purse or wallet or in your pocket
- A pen with gold ink
- A white candle in a stable candleholder
- Matches
- A stick of frankincense
- A piece of black silk big enough to wrap around the card

When should I do this spell?
On a Saturday after dark

What should I do?
Draw the following letters in gold on the card, forming a square:

S	A	T	O	R
A	R	E	P	O
T	E	N	E	T
O	P	E	R	A
R	O	T	A	S

A rough translation for the words would be "Sator, sower of the seed, spins the wheel," which can be interpreted to mean that when a human being expends some effort in the direction of a true goal, the universe will match the effort and the goal will be achieved.

Once you have drawn the talisman, light the candle, and hold the talisman in your hand in the candle's light. Burn the frankincense incense and pass the talisman repeatedly through the smoke to bless and cleanse it.

Improvise a sincere prayer to King Solomon asking for protection against all harm. Wrap the talisman in a piece of black silk and carry it on you for as long as you feel the need for protection.

TIME-STRETCHING SPELLS

The following spell will help you "stretch" time. Often, even when we think we are concentrating hard on the task at hand, our minds are actually wandering off to different thoughts, some of which may be negative. This spell will help you focus on the activity you are working on, and will make you feel that you have all the time in the world. In Native American traditions it is believed that people create time, and are not just swept along with the time stream.

What do I need?
• A white candle in a stable candleholder
• Matches
• A clock with a second hand

When should I do this spell?
Whenever you need more time to finish your studies

What should I do?
This spell only takes about ten minutes, so you should have enough time to do this spell and still get your work done. You can do this spell at your desk. Light the candle and position the clock so that you can see it from your chair.

Sit in your chair and focus on your breathing. Deepen your breathing—breathe in for a count of four and out for a count of four. Watch the flame of the candle and allow your mind to let go of all your thoughts. Close your eyes and "see" the image of the candle flame floating in front of your eyes.

Consciously move the image of the flame so that it is in the middle of your forehead. This visualization will help open your intuitive capabilities, which will help you with your work once you start up again.

In this calm state, open your eyes, look at the clock and watch the second hand go all the way around the clock face—feel each second as it passes. Keep that awareness of time stretching out and slowing down before you until you finish your project. You can keep the candle burning while you do your work if you feel it helps.

TRUE BEAUTY SPELL

True, long-lasting success often comes from self-awareness, from a deep knowledge of our own true worth. Try this spell whenever you feel down or have had a rough day. Also use this spell before going to a job interview or asking for a pay raise or promotion. The herb used in this spell is fennel, which is renowned for its ability to protect against negative energies and aid meditation. A clear quartz crystal is often used in spell craft because these crystals can store your thoughts or the intentions of your spell.

What do I need?
• A bunch of fresh fennel
• A clear quartz crystal

When should I do this spell?
Anytime

What should I do?
Shape the fennel into a closely packed nest onto which you can set your crystal.
Sit in a comfortable position with the fennel and crystal nest in front of you. Smell the fresh fennel and concentrate on the crystal. Visualize the crystal being energized with pure joy. Imagine what pure joy would feel like while you look at the crystal.

Pick up the crystal and imagine the stone literally throbbing with the energy of pure joy. Hold the crystal and let its energy surround you. Now think of who you are. Use only positive and loving terms. Feel that you are a good and truly beautiful person.

When you feel ready, take three deep breaths and place the crystal back on its nest of fennel. Carry this crystal with you when you are expecting a difficult day and when you feel the need for extra support.

TRUE LOVE SPELLS

WHAT IS THE NAME OF MY TRUE LOVE?

There are a great many traditional spells for finding out the name of your true lover. After casting this spell, you may be surprised by the name that comes through.

What do I need?

- Four drops of rose geranium essential oil
- A tea light
- An oil burner
- Matches
- A metal bowl to catch the shavings
- An apple
- A sharp paring knife

When should I do this spell?

On a Friday

What should I do?

Measure out the essential oil, light the oil burner, and sit in a comfortable chair with the bowl at your feet and the knife and the apple beside you. Place the oil burner near you so that you can smell the scent and see the tea light burning.

Focus on the scent of the essential oil and feel your mind tuning into finding out the name of your true love. Pick up the apple and the paring knife and say:

With this knife I shall carve out the first letter of
  my true love's name.

Peel the apple—with your right hand if you are right-handed and your left hand if you are left-handed. Try to keep the line of the peel unbroken as long as possible. When the peel breaks, let it land in the bowl.

See if the shape in which the peel has fallen forms a letter. Even if you cannot discern a letter, concentrate on the shape of the peel. The first name that pops into your head will be the name of your true love.

WHAT WILL MY TRUE LOVE BE LIKE?

This spell focuses on encouraging your dreams to give you a picture of what your true love is like. It includes a charm that you can speak before you go to sleep. This charm will help your subconscious give you a clue as to your true love's qualities, and perhaps a clue to his or her identity.

What do I need?

- A piece of parchment paper
- Your favorite pen
- A piece of red ribbon
- A piece of red fabric
- A journal or your spell journal (see pages 154–155)

When should I do this spell?

On a Friday evening just before you go to sleep

What should I do?

On the sheet of parchment paper, write the following charm:

The face, the form, the touch, the voice,
The love to make my heart rejoice.
The name and nature unconcealed;
My love, in dreams, shall be revealed.

—LIAM CYFRIN

When you have memorized the charm, roll up the paper tightly and tie it with the red ribbon. Wrap it in red cloth and put it under your pillow. Place your journal and pen near you, perhaps on the bedside table, and when you wake up, write down what you can remember of your dreams.

These dreams will give you clues to what your true love will be like. Write down all the details you can remember, even ones that seem irrelevant. These may turn out to be the most important clues of all. See also pages 117–118 for a mirror spell and a herb spell that will help you see your true love.

U

UNWANTED ATTENTION PROTECTION

AVOIDING UNWANTED ATTENTIONS SPELL

When faced with demands from an unwanted suitor or
unwelcomed advances from a stranger, you need to rely on your
inner strength, and to realize that you have the power to say "No."

In these situations it is better to use your common sense than
lash out and be unkind or mean. The latter solution only indicates
that you are feeling fearful and are not in control of the situation.
Any unkindness you show is likely to rebound on you threefold.
The following spell will give you an extra edge when confronted
with unwanted attentions.

What do I need?

• Some visualization skills

When should I do this spell?

Anytime you feel threatened

What should I do?

When you are faced with unwanted attention, immediately ground
yourself. Become conscious of the energy of the ground under your
feet. Imagine a blue line of energy moving from the ground through
your feet, then through your body and up through your head.
Imagine this blue line expanding out until it encloses you within its
glow. Keep this image in your head all the time you are talking to
your unwanted suitor or being watched by an unsavory character.

Feel that the blue, safe cocoon that you have created around
yourself is a cloak with a deep hood; it completely covers you and
allows you to move quickly and silently.

Watch the reactions of the other person. When the person's eyes
start sliding away from you, as if they are having trouble focusing
on you, it is time to politely leave. When you are ready, earth the
blue light back into the ground. Imagine the cloak compressing into
a blue line that travels back down into the ground. Don't forget to
do this—if you don't do it, you will soon be wondering why your
friends are not talking to you.

A CHARM TO DISCOURAGE UNWANTED ATTENTION

Sometimes we seem to be highly appealing to someone even though we are already happily involved in a loving relationship. Unwanted attention like this often makes us feel uncomfortable, and can even create difficulties in our present relationship.

The following spell is said to discourage unwanted advances very effectively. The power of the spell centers on making a special "go away" powder that will not harm the person in any way.

What do I need?

- A photograph of the person you wish to discourage
- A dab of butter or oil
- A piece of dark-colored cloth big enough to wrap the photograph in
- A teaspoon of chili powder
- A teaspoon of black pepper
- A teaspoon of paprika powder
- A teaspoon of cayenne pepper
- A saucepan
- A small glass jar with a lid
- A red candle in a stable candleholder
- Matches
- Three sugar cubes

When should I do this spell?

Anytime you feel troubled by unwanted advances or during the phase of the waning moon

What should I do?

Take the photograph and smear it with butter or oil, then wrap it in the cloth and set it aside. Next, place the powders and the peppers in a saucepan on a stove and dry roast the spices for a brief moment over very high heat, being careful not to burn them. When the spices have cooled, place the mixture in a jar. This is your "go away" powder. Place the wrapped up photograph on the floor in front of you. Remove its dark "shroud" and place the candle and candleholder next to it. Sprinkle the "go away" powder in a circle around the photograph, light the candle and whisper the following thirteen times:

Go from me hence and find thee another.

Leave the charm until the candle has burned out, then take the photograph to running water (a stream or canal) and toss it in, closely followed by three sugar cubes. The spell is done.

VISUALIZATIONS AND SPELLS

SEE ALSO **MIND POWER AND SPELLS** ON PAGE 133.

Visualization is an essential spell craft technique. Spells may be regarded as the key to unlocking a form of powerful energy that can be directed toward a desired result. The ability to feel magic working, and to direct it by visualizing the exact outcome you would like, can weave more potent magic than using precisely the right spell ingredients will.

A successful spell is like a journey; the ingredients and actions are the vehicle, intuition is the map, visualization is the fuel, and the outcome is the arrival.

When you visualize the outcome of a spell in fine detail and experience the joy of success before the outcome has occurred, you are letting the universe know what you would like in your life. The universe is often very accommodating of your goals when you know what is best for yourself. At the end of every spell, and for as long as it takes afterward, imagine the outcome you would like in as much detail as possible.

SPELL CRAFT TIP

Flying your broomstick—an exercise in visualization

Visualizing flying a broomstick is a fun way of getting into the mood of your spell and allowing yourself to believe that anything is possible! Experienced magical practitioners are thought to be able to project their spirit, or astral body, and fly in real time to where they wish to go. This is called astral projection. Astral projection or astral travel is a very advanced technique—it should not be attempted by someone just starting out in magic. It is thought that dreams are sometimes memories of astral travels.

Fear of failure and pessimism are forms of visualizing an outcome that all too often attract misfortune. Make a pact with yourself that for at least three weeks, starting when you perform your spell, you will suspend disbelief, replace negativity with positive thoughts, and look forward to achieving your goal.

Remember, if your spell is not successful, it means the universe has decided, in its wisdom, that your goal is not beneficial to you—something far better is in store for you.

Visualization is very simple: if you can dream and imagine, you can visualize. The basic difference is that when you are visualizing, you must fully believe that you can achieve the goal in your mind, and that it can be empowered by a continuing stream of positive thoughts.

GETTING INTO THE MOOD: SOME VISUALIZATION EXERCISES

If you notice that your mind starts to wander when you are trying to visualize the success of your spell, it might be a good idea to do a few visualization exercises to improve your skills. Also, if the spell is for yourself, you might be subconsciously sabotaging your spell by feeling in some way unworthy of success. Take time to acknowledge and understand any misgivings you may have about the success you seek. If you are not one hundred percent behind your spell, it is not likely to work. This is sometimes why even experienced spell casters ask a trusted friend to do a certain spell for them.

Visualization exercises are simple, but they do take a great deal of concentration and perseverance.

One exercise is to try focusing on a photograph of a landscape, noticing all the details in the photograph, even the shape of the trees. Once you feel confident that you know the picture well, tear the photograph in half. Put one half on the table in front of you and try to visualize the other half.

An advanced exercise is to visualize a piece of fruit using all your senses—see the fruit, touch it, smell it, eat it, and hear the sound it makes as you bite into it.

WATER OF PLENTY SPELL

Magical waters are extensively used in the magic traditions of the Caribbean and the United States, where they are sold by mail order and in retail outlets servicing the magically minded. These waters are given exotic names and are intended for use in bath, wash, and scrub water.

What do I need?

- A handful of cinnamon powder
- A small handful of allspice or pimento powder
- A handful of dried basil leaves
- A handful of dried mint leaves
- The rind of an orange
- A dash of sugar
- A large saucepan filled with water
- A strainer

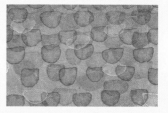

- A bottle (with a lid) that is big enough to hold the potion
- Ten coins of small denomination
- A cup of alcohol (ordinary household alcohol such as methylated spirit may be used)
- A teaspoon of green food dye

When should I do this spell?

On a Thursday evening

What should I do?

Place all ingredients except the alcohol and food dye in the saucepan filled with water. Bring the liquid to a boil, then reduce the heat and let it simmer for half an hour, topping up the liquid if necessary (the final amount should be the same as the amount you started with). Set the saucepan aside to cool. When the liquid is cool, strain it into the bottle. Add the coins, the alcohol, and the food dye and close the bottle's lid. This mixture is Water of Plenty potion. Add a quarter cup of the potion to your bath and to the wash to draw the energies of prosperity to you, your home, and the members of your household. Shake the bottle well before each use.

WILL THIS RELATIONSHIP LAST SPELL

One of the important aspects of magic is that when you cast spells, you are accepting responsibility for the direction you want your life to go in. Whether a relationship will last is truly within your own control. The spell below will help you tap into your own instincts and guide you toward enjoying the relationship you have or finding one that will suit you even better.

What do I need?

• An oil burner
• A tea light
• Matches
• Four drops of cinnamon essential oil
• The Lovers card, a major arcana card from your favorite tarot deck
• Your journal

When should I do this spell?

Friday evening

What should I do?

Gather your tools and ingredients in a safe and comfortable place where you will not be disturbed. Set up the oil burner, tea light, matches, and cinnamon essential oil. Light the candle and breathe in the scent of cinnamon.Focus on your breathing and feel yourself let go of your daily worries. Focus on the Lovers card. Allow yourself to examine the image on the card in great detail. Feel as if you are falling into the image.

In this relaxed state of mind, ask the following question:

What do I need to do to make this relationship last for
the benefit of both myself and [insert name]?

Continue looking at the card and listen for or watch, in a detached manner, any message, advice, or images that come into your mind. Write these down in your journal. Do not analyze them—just keep writing until you feel ready to stop, then immediately close your journal.

Take three deep breaths and turn the tarot card face down. Open your journal and start to sift through the information. You may be surprised by the clues you have been given. Above all, honor what your intuition has told you.

WINNING THE GAME

This is a fun spell to help you and your team win a game. It presupposes that the game involves a ball—anything from a football to a tennis ball. If your sport involves other equipment instead, see if you can adapt the spell to suit your game.

What do I need?

- Two circles of fabric or soft leather to make a miniature version of the ball used in your sport
- A needle, and thread that matches the leather in color
- A tablespoon of each of the following:
  sea salt, cinnamon, pepper, lemon balm, thyme
- A piece of garnet
- A piece of jade (optional)
- A small snippet of your hair, or a stray thread from your sports clothes, or ribbons/pure wool representing the colors of your team, plus padding from you or the team

When should I do this spell?

On the night before the game

What should I do?

The night before the game, make the ball by sewing the outer edges of two circles of fabric or leather, leaving an opening so that you turn the circle inside out. Try to make the ball look as much like the ball you use in the game as possible. At least make it the same color. For example, use orange for a basketball, yellow for a tennis ball, or red for a cricket ball.

Clip the seam and turn the fabric inside out. To make the circle a sphere, stuff it with the salt and the herbs. Each ingredient has energy that will be useful for helping you win the game:

sea salt—protection against negative energies
cinnamon—focus and communication
pepper—protection and quick footedness
lemon balm—healing and avoiding injury
thyme—courage and wisdom.

Put in the garnet, which corresponds to the energy of courage, and a piece of jade if there is a cash prize for winning the game. Stuff in the hair, thread, ribbons or wool, and padding and sew the opening shut. Take this ball with you to the game and let the powers blended within it help you win the game.

WISHING WELL SPELL

You don't have to have landscape gardening skills to cast this
spell! Just use a vase and some small polished river stones to cast a
decorative as well as effective ongoing spell.

What do I need?

- A wide, deep, clear vase
- A handful of clean, polished pebbles
- A couple of tiny, pretty cut flowers or
  some shells
- Water to cover the pebbles in the vase
- A silver-colored coin

When should I do this spell?

During the phase of the full moon

What should I do?

Arrange the polished pebbles in your
vase so that it looks like a pretty pool.
Put the cut flowers between the
pebbles—it will look like a naturally occurring forest stream now. If
you have some shells that you like to use, add them instead, to
make the vase and pebbles look like a rock pool. Do not use flowers
and shells together. Pour enough water into the bowl to cover the
pebbles and flowers or shells.

Place the vase so that the light of the moon will shine on the
water. Just before you go to sleep, throw the silver coin into the pool
and make a wish. Make the wish a quick one, so that you have
finished saying what you want before the coin hits the bottom of
the pool.

Put your hand in the water and, without disturbing the coin,
pick up a pebble from the bottom of the pool. Hold it in your hand
and say your wish again. Make sure you use the same words. Dry
the pebble and slip it under your pillow. Be mindful of your dreams
that night—you will dream of how your wish will come true or
what you need to do to make your wish happen.

When you wake up, throw the water out of the vase. Collect the
pebbles, and the flowers or shells, and dry them, perhaps putting
the pebbles and shells in your special spell box. If you used flowers,
put them in a small silver vase and put the vase in the window
where you put the spell vase. The spell is done.

WORK SPELLS

JOB ACKNOWLEDGMENT SPELL

There are times when you just can't seem to get the recognition that you deserve; if you do your work well, it is easy to be taken for granted. This spell features a name charm which can be used to subtly heighten the awareness of your name in the workplace.

What do I need?
- A strip of parchment paper about 6 in. long and 2 in. wide
- A red pen
- A piece of red ribbon long enough to tie the piece of paper when it is rolled up
- A sprig of rosemary

When should I do this spell?
During the phase of the new moon

What should I do?
When you are on a break at work, write down your name repeatedly on the strip of paper until one side is covered with your name. It is important to use a red pen.

Roll up the piece of paper and tie it with the ribbon. Tuck the sprig of rosemary (if you are at work you are going to have to bring this to work with you) between the ribbon and the paper.

If you work at a desk, place the paper in front of you, at the top end of your desk. If this part of your desk is cluttered, tidy it up. In feng shui, this section of your desk corresponds to fame and acknowledgment. The spell is done.

GETTING A PROMOTION

In busy organizations, promotions are sometimes overlooked as everyone is frantically trying to meet their deadlines or stick to their budgets, so being overlooked does not necessarily mean that your workplace does not value you.

Regardless of why you now need to ask for a promotion, try the following spell to tap into the planetary powers of Mars and Mercury, which will help you get the support you need to gain a promotion.

What do I need?

- A pinch of each of the following:
  coriander powder
  cumin powder
  curry powder
  ground black cracked pepper
  ground tarragon
  tobacco
  caraway seeds
  ground coffee
- Three tablespoons of the juice from an aloe vera plant
- A small amber-colored glass jar with a screw-top lid
- A small metal spoon

When should I do this spell?

On a Tuesday or a Wednesday

What should I do?

Place all the ingredients in the jar, measuring out the dried ingredients first and then pouring in the aloe vera juice. It is best if the aloe vera juice has been collected that morning.

With the spoon, stir the ingredients together, visualizing yourself asking for a promotion. Imagine feeling strong and in control. When you feel ready, screw the lid onto the jar and take it to work with you.

Aloe vera and amber correspond to success, and the herbs are plants that correspond to Mars and Mercury. Mars is responsible for giving you courage and Mercury gives you the eloquence to state your case.

JOB INTERVIEW SPELL

Feng shui has a number of useful tips on how to succeed at a job interview. This spell weaves Eastern and Western mysteries together to help you succeed. To enhance the flow of beneficial energy to you during your job interview, make sure that your back is not facing the door of the interview room. If the chair is positioned for you to sit that way, move it a little so that you are facing the doorway.

What do I need?
- A clean, soft cloth
- A sprig of fresh rosemary
- A black tassel

When should I do this spell?
Sometime before your appointment on the day of the interview

What should I do?
On the morning of your interview, clear all the money, papers, and other items out of your wallet, purse, briefcase, or handbag. Take the cloth and clean out any accumulated lint and dust. This is symbolic of clearing out old negative energy.

Put back only the necessary items and make sure that everything is neat and clean. Place the sprig of rosemary in your briefcase or handbag and tie the black tassel to the handles. If you don't want the tassel to show, carry it in your pocket.

Rosemary is an excellent herb to protect you from a negative response to your application. It also helps stimulate your memory, so that you won't forget your preparation for the interview. Tassels are used to disperse negative energy and the color black symbolizes strength and perseverance.

JOB LOSS PROTECTION SPELL

There may be times in your working life when you feel less than safe about the security of your job. The following spell is based on feng shui principles and will help protect you against negative energies that may be affecting your physical presence at the workplace.

What do I need?

- A mirror
- A trophy (not necessarily related to your work; a trophy for a sporting event that you won when you were a child would be suitable)
- A black pen
- A piece of paper small enough to paste underneath the paperweight
- A paperweight

When should I do this spell?

During the phase of the new moon

What should I do?

Place the mirror right in front of you as you sit at your desk or workstation. Put the trophy in front of the mirror. This creates the magical illusion that you have double the trophies. You are also anchoring the image of the trophy to the reflection of yourself in the mirror.

With your black pen write the words "Secure Job" on the piece of paper. Paste the paper on the underside of the paperweight and place the paperweight on top of any paperwork or important files you are currently working on, or simply put it on your desk or workstation near your right elbow. The weight of the paperweight is thought to symbolize how hard it would be to shift out of your job.

Make sure you deconstruct this spell by removing the paperweight from your desk when you want to cast a spell for a promotion—otherwise, the energy around you may keep you stuck in the job you're in at a time when you may want to move on!

WORLD PEACE SPELLS

SENDING PROTECTIVE ENERGY TO THE WORLD SPELL

This is a big spell and should be done by a large group. The spell combines symbols of East and West to direct protective energy toward helping the world stay in balance.

What do we need?

- A heavy stone
- A thick candle
- A tall "garden" incense stick or four usual-sized incense sticks
- A cauldron of water
- The mask of a dragon
- Matches
- A flower
- A black marker pen
- Rainbow-colored streamers for everyone participating in the spell

When should we do this spell?

During the phase of the full moon

What should we do?

In a natural clearing, scratch out a circle that will accommodate the number of people who are casting the spell. Quarter the circle and place the stone and candle at opposite ends to each other. Position the incense stick or sticks and the cauldron of water in the two remaining quarters. Gather everyone in the circle and choose one person to lead the spell and carry the dragon's mask. A separate person should be chosen to, in this order, light the incense stick, light the candle, drop the flower in the water, and draw an upright pentagram on the stone with the pen.

Next, pick up the stone and carry it to the center of the circle. If you are leading the spell, put on the dragon's mask and start running, jumping, and dancing around the inside of the circle, running in among the people of the circle, getting them to follow you, holding their streamers out from their bodies. Continue the dancing until you feel the energy starting to peak.

At this point, move to the stone and touch it, pouring the raised energy back into the earth and saying:

We direct this energy back to you, for your will, your protection, and your balance. So mote it be.

Get everyone to put their hands onto the earth. The spell is done.

A SPELL FOR WORLD PEACE

The following spell is a method of tapping into the stream of universal peace energy and making your own little piece of the world brighter by nullifying negative energy.

What do I need?

• A white candle
• Matches
• A blue bead or marble
• A white feather
• A small jar of spring or filtered water sweetened with sugar

When should I do this spell?

During the phase of the full moon

What should I do?

Light the candle, turn off any artificial illumination, and arrange all your spell items in front of you. Sit for a moment and still your mind.

Hold the bead or marble in your hand and feel the fragility of the Earth in the hands of humanity; feel the destructive potential of greed and fear. Blow a cool stream of breath on the bead or marble.

Dip the white feather into the water and use it as a paintbrush to bathe the marble or bead in water, symbolically cooling the anger of war and destruction with the feather of peace.

Place the bead or marble in the jar of water and visualize the world spinning slowly in a bank of beautiful billowing clouds. Put the jar in a cool, quiet part of your home where it will not be disturbed. Put the feather underneath your bed and let the candle burn out by itself.

Here the spell ends but the true work begins: in your daily life, practice the art of releasing and ending cycles of fear and destruction.

INDEX

Thunder Bay Press
An imprint of the Advantage Publishers Group
5880 Oberlin Drive, San Diego, CA 92121-4794
www.thunderbaybooks.com

All notations of errors or omissions should be addressed to Thunder Bay Press, Editorial Department, at the above address. All other correspondence (author inquiries, permissions) concerning the content of this book should be addressed to Lansdowne Publishing, Level 1, 18 Argyle Street, The Rocks NSW 2000, Australia.

ISBN 1-57145-997-9
Library of Congress Cataloging-in-Publication Data available on request.

Set in Birka and LT Ergo on QuarkXPress
Printed in Singapore by Tien Wah Press (Pte) Ltd
1 2 3 4 5   07 06 05 04 03